*Complete Cross-Country
Skiing and Ski Touring*

D0066685

Complete Cross-Country

Skiing and Ski Touring

by WILLIAM J. LEDERER and JOE PETE WILSON

Illustrations by Frank Thomas

Revised Edition

 W. W. NORTON & COMPANY, INC., New York

Contents

Part IV—Waxing and the Wind-Chill Factor

Introduction

I, Bill Lederer, took up cross-country skiing at the age of fifty-six. I had drifted into skiing haphazardly, buying my second-hand equipment at an auction. The total cost for skis, bindings, boots, and poles was eleven dollars. Putting them on, catch-as-catch-can, I went out on the snow and began fooling around.

Whatever was possible to do wrong, I did wrong. Beginning then, I have fallen into just about every square inch of snow in Caledonia County, Vermont. But I never got hurt—not at all —and I had great fun.

The day I first skied the several miles to the village for mail because the snowplow was late getting through was the day that cross-country became a passion of mine. I knew I had to learn how to do it properly. I bought every book on the market. Many were excellent, but they were written, it seemed, mostly for those who wanted to go into competition racing. I had no desire to get into competition racing—I just wanted to tour the countryside, relax, and enjoy myself.

I realized that I would have to find a professional instructor. I began asking every cross-country skier I met, "Who is the best teacher?" The name Joe Pete Wilson was mentioned so often by so many people that I decided Joe Pete was the teacher for me.

It was a happy surprise when I discovered that he lived near me in Vermont's Northeast Kingdom.

After the first lesson (in which he taught me to bend my knees), I felt like a tiger and began to ski terrain which had previously frightened me. After several lessons from patient and skillful Joe Pete, I had a hankering to ski tour with the local experts; and, to my astonishment, I was able to do so.

Better yet, Joe Pete and I became warm friends and we went out on some long and wild cross-country tours together. Of course, I am not in his league (he was an Olympic Cross-Country Team member), but with a lot of huffing, puffing, and laughter (and with him slowing down generously from time to time), I managed to tag along.

The fact that I am middle-aged, not particularly athletic, had had no previous skiing experience, and had still learned how to get around fairly well on skis fascinated both Joe Pete and me. If I could learn, couldn't *anyone* learn cross-country skiing?

We wondered if a method could be developed for teaching cross-country to *anyone*—old or young, experienced or inexperienced. We formed a partnership to find out.

We held a series of cross-country clinics for beginners. We experimented to find out what kind of people could learn the sport and how quickly. Joe Pete supplied the technical know-how and I judged the pace and terminology suited to novices.

Most of our students had never seen cross-country skis before. A good percentage of our skiers were fiftyish and out of shape.

We assumed that our students wanted to ski primarily for *fun*, at least at first (perhaps some would go on to race), and for that sense of physical well-being which usually comes after a cross-country tour. We also assumed that they did not come to our clinics in the hope of becoming Olympic cross-country champions that year.

After four hours of the first clinic (which covered about the same material as Part I of this book), we tried what we thought was rather a risk. We took our sixty-three novices out on a three-mile ski tour. Fourteen of them were between fifty and seventy years of age; eleven were in their late teens or early twenties.

To our surprise, almost all of the novices finished the three-mile tour, and all had fun.

We learned that although middle-aged novices did not have the rapid reflexes of the teen-agers, they were able to apply techniques almost as quickly—*provided they learned the first, basic lesson slowly and well.* Of course, the teen-agers were able to move along the snow at a faster pace during that first tour. Also, they had a better sense of balance during the downhill runs.

But, in some instances, the middle-aged skiers—because of their more relaxed pace and high motivation (to show that middle-age isn't so bad after all)—were able to go longer distances and with less noticeable fatigue than the younger people.

In some cases, the older skiers *seemed* to have a higher stamina factor than the kids. It may have been due to the fact that the older people were laughing more and accepting the cross-country touring as *fun*, not as the grimly serious, competitive action which often stimulates teen-agers. Perhaps it came from psychological stimulus, resulting from the "stay young" obsession which seems to belong uniquely to our culture.

In any case, we have sufficient data to show that the surprisingly high stamina factor of many middle-aged skiers is a fact and not just coincidence.

At the end of each experimental clinic, our new cross-country skiers were delighted and surprised with their success. Many requested tapes of our spoken lessons. We decided it would be more effective to write a small book.

We were also influenced by the fact that, although *cross-country skiing is the fastest-growing sport in the country*, there are not many professional cross-country instructors available. One can usually find them only at a few resorts and at the excellent clinics scheduled by the Ski Touring Council.°

For us two cross-country ski bums (one a happy, middle-aged amateur and one a happy, thirty-five-year-old professional), writing about cross-country skiing was a source of much pleasure. We hope that the readers will get as much joy from the book as we got from writing it.

Part I of this book is for beginners who don't know a cross-country ski from a ladder. Part II is for novices intent on becoming intermediates. Part III is for those who now feel completely at home on cross-country skis and want to let loose with the experts. Part IV deals with the all-important matter of waxing.

We don't promise to get anyone on the United States Olympic Team; but we feel confident that no matter how young or how old the skier-to-be is, he will soon feel comfortable on cross-country skis and will enjoy the pleasures of ski touring—or even racing, if so inclined.

° Complete information on ski touring, trails, clinics, and clubs can be obtained by sending $2.00 to Rudolph F. Mattesich, President, Ski Touring Council, Inc., West Hill Road, Troy, Vermont, 05868. We recommend this for all ski tourers.

PART I

BEGINNING

1

What Is Cross-Country Skiing?

What is cross-country skiing (the general sport also known as ski touring, Nordic skiing, and XC)?

First, we will tell you what cross-country skiing is *not*.

Cross-country skiing is not the same as alpine (often called downhill) skiing. In alpine skiing, the skier is lifted up the side of the mountain by engine-powered equipment. He has to use the lift because his equipment is too rigid and too heavy to allow him to ascend to the top by using his own muscles. His skiing, therefore, is restricted to those resorts which have ski lifts. And, in the majority of cases, even the snow has to be prepared beforehand by expensive mechanical equipment.

As soon as he reaches the top, the skier races down the

snowy slopes as fast as he can or dares. After having completed his run, he stands in line and waits to be lifted up to the summit again.

On a weekend at many alpine resorts, the downhill skier spends six hours per day on the slopes, but only gets in about ninety minutes of actual skiing. The rest of the time is spent buying lift tickets, waiting in line, riding the lifts, getting warmed up, or eating. For this, he spends a minimum of twenty dollars a day.

Today, alpine skiing is big business, grossing several billion dollars annually. It is well advertised; and for the last few years, it has been the "in" sport, fashionable and expensive. To spend six hundred dollars for alpine ski equipment and clothes is not unusual.

Alpine skiing, of course, is melodramatic, fast, and dangerous. It is the speed and hazards which excite people.

A downhill run takes only a few minutes. In that brief interval, there frequently can be, and are, serious accidents.

Cross-country skiing (XC) is very different. It is one of the oldest activities in the world. Archeological evidence indicates that cross-country is over five thousand years old. For millennia in Scandinavia, it has been the major means of winter transport. People traveled from town to town, from home to store, to and from school—everywhere—on cross-country skis. They still do.

Basically, cross-country is traveling over snow on inexpensive wooden skis. Little else is needed; and the skier can go wherever he wishes—uphill, downhill, or on the flats. By skiing cross-country he can travel over snow faster than by any other means—except, of course, by snow mobile. (One advantage of cross-country skiing is that it provides an escape from the snow mobile, since the cross-country skier can tour where the snow mobile cannot.)

There are many reasons for the sudden growth in the popularity of cross-country skiing.

It is a safe, natural sport. Anyone who can walk can learn to ski tour. Wherever a person can walk in the summer, there he can ski in the winter.

The skier has the satisfaction of getting around the countryside on his own. He is free of roads and alone.

A person touring on cross-country skis is independent of mechanical needs. Unlike alpine skiing, there is no lift, no line to wait in, no ticket to buy, and no long auto, plane, or bus trip to take in order to reach a prepared area.

Wherever there is snow, the cross-country skier can travel. Joe Pete Wilson has skied across the tundras of Finland, across the wilds of Alaska, hundreds of miles from any house, as well as in the well-prepared tracks of Olympic competition. I have skied two and a half miles down Fifth Avenue to make a 7:30 A.M. appointment following a big blizzard. My son, Jon, has skied along the banks of the Charles River, one block from Harvard University. All three of us have skied in our backyards in Vermont, in Central Park, and on various golf courses.

For us—and apparently for a growing number of others— there is a unique sense of well-being in cross-country skiing. In the snowy hills there is the soothing quality of silence and the relief of being free from the many restrictions of modern civilization.

The body benefits from the use of many muscles at a pace and vigor of the skier's choice.

Cross-country can be a "loner" sport for the individual who needs occasional solitude.

It also can be a wonderful family and group sport for those interested in "togetherness." Cross-country is one of the few activities left in our culture in which all of the family members can go out together (from grandparents down to small children) and perform as equals.

In Oslo, it is common to see trainloads of families riding out ten, fifteen, or even twenty miles—and then, as a family, skiing home together.

Anyone who can walk can cross-country ski!

2

Beginner's Check-Off Equipment List

There is such a variety of XC equipment on the market that the beginner should have professional counsel before spending any money on the boots, skis, poles, and clothing which later will become very precious to him.

What follows is *specific* advice.

We want the skier-to-be to get on the snow with the most functional gear, and to learn to ski and have fun. The equipment we recommend will be functional for the beginner and will still do well for him after he becomes an expert (although by then he may wish for a bit of variety).

For cross-country skiing (XC), the following are needed: skis; ski boots, which are really light, flexible, leather shoes that go up just over the ankle; ski bindings to fasten the boots to the skis; ski poles; a ski-waxing outfit; and heavy winter socks, body clothing, and gloves or mittens (which, of course, most people already own).

Skis (What Type to Buy)

Type of ski: The general touring ski (not the light touring ski; *Fig. 1*).

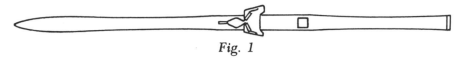

Fig. 1

Length of ski: From 8 to 12 inches longer than the skier's height. (When the arm is held straight over the head, the ski should reach the wrist.)

Material: Wood, with either birch or hickory bottoms. (*Note:* There are excellent skis with plastic bottoms; but we recommend that the beginner *not* start with them. They are more difficult to wax, more difficult in certain snow conditions, and more expensive.)

Width of ski: Between 2½ to 3 inches. The width should be measured near the tip or tail of the ski. The middle of the ski will be about 2 to 2½ inches wide.

Weight: About six pounds for a general touring ski.

Construction: (a) Laminated, which permits essential springiness (the best skis have from twenty to thirty-two laminations); and (b) camber (a slight bow-shape). If put flat on the floor, the ski rests on its tip and tail, with the middle off the floor. The skier should make certain that both skis have equal camber. When he stands on the skis, they should be flat over their entire length. (*Note:* Camber is built into the ski so that the skier's weight is evenly distributed over the entire length of ski. Also, it provides some of the flexibility needed for uneven terrain.)

Edges: It is not necessary for beginners to own skis with edges; but the majority of modern, moderately priced skis have them. Edges should be hickory, compressed beechwood, or plastic (*Fig. 2*).

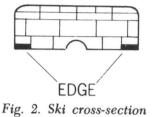

EDGE

Fig. 2. Ski cross-section

Price: At the time of this writing, the price of general touring skis varies from fifteen to fifty dollars. Buy the lowest-priced ski which has the laminations, camber, and either birch or hickory bottoms.

Preparation of bottom: One should ask the store to prepare the ski bottoms the first time. This involves "burning in" a tar compound (see pages 168–172).

Notes: If the beginner is a young skier who intends to take up competitive cross-country racing, then he should start off with skis from the middle price range, with hickory bottoms, about 2 5/16 inches maximum width (measured near tip and tail), and weighing about 4 lbs. 3 ozs. (Such skis are slightly narrower than regular touring skis and produce less drag. Since races are almost always held on a prepared or "hard" track, the narrower ski is suitable. But such skis break more easily than the regular touring skis.)

There is a new product of interest to "recreational skiers" —the No-wax [tm] ski. The bottom is of hard plastic molded into a fish-scale pattern. The "bite" of the fish-scale bottom makes moving ahead simple for beginners, especially when going uphill. Also, the base requires no preparation or waxing. For the recreational skier who goes out on friendly snow and who does not wish to learn the art of waxing, the No-wax [tm] can be a tremendous boon. It is also convenient, for a skier of any level, when there is a variety of snow conditions on the trail or track —warm sunshine on some sections of snow and cold shade on others, which might require a change of wax. We found the ski particularly good in higher temperatures, when the snow was wet and mushy.

On cold, new snow, the No-wax ^{tm} is not as fast as a well waxed wooden ski, and it performs badly on ice (where the wooden ski would be using a klister). But under about 80 percent of snow conditions, the No-wax ^{tm} is a convenient piece of equipment. Do not be alarmed by the "singing" sound these skis make going downhill. It is a harmonic sound created by the fish-scales on the bottom.

The Binding

Toe-Clamp Binding

The binding is the metal device that holds the toe of the boot securely to the ski.

Contrary to the belief held by many United States cross-country ski instructors and ski shopowners, we strongly recommend that the beginner start off with the toe-clamp binding

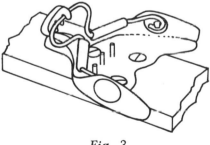

Fig. 3

(*Fig.* 3). This is usually associated only with racing and is frequently misnamed a racing binding simply because racers use it. The toe-clamp binding is also known under the trade name of Rottefella. Except for mountaineering skiing, we believe that the toe-clamp binding is the best all-round type (see illustration).

The toe-clamp binding holds the boot to the ski by means of clamp pressure on the front of the boot sole, and by means of several tiny metal nipples which protrude upward from the binding about a quarter of an inch. These metal nipples fit into three or more eyelets in the sole of the boot just in front of the ball of the foot (advanced skiers sometimes use rubber-soled boots that will fit any combination of nipples).

The toe-clamp binding is recommended by us because:

(1) It is by far the simplest binding. There is nothing that can slip out of alignment and require readjustment.

(2) A skier wearing boots having the eyelets in the soles can immediately use any pair of skis having a toe-clamp binding. With other types of binding, this is usually impossible without making adjustments requiring a screw driver and frequently a wrench or pliers.

(3) Toe-clamp bindings are the least expensive ones.

(4) The toe clamp provides the most toe and ankle flexibility.

(5) Toe-clamp bindings are less tiring to ski in. For example, because the toe-clamp binding is the most flexible, the skier can most easily pick himself up after a fall.

(6) The toe-clamp binding is easier and quicker to get into and out of. On a cold day, this added ease becomes much appreciated.

There are instructors who claim that beginners, especially middle-aged novices, should not get the toe-clamp binding. The reason offered is that the cable-around-heel binding (usually called the Tempo- or Jofa-type binding, after their trade names) gives more support to the ankle than does the toe-clamp binding.

Our experiments indicate that this is true if the new skier does not learn proper techniques for traversing, turning, and weight shifting. If he learns the correct techniques, we believe that the toe-clamp binding is superior in almost every way to the cable-around-heel type.

Our professional friends in Scandinavia, experts who teach cross-country skiing in Norway and Sweden, agree with us. Today, the toe-clamp binding is used by most Scandinavians for cross-country touring. The exception, of course, is mountaineering skiing, which is another breed of sport.

It is almost impossible to make a mistake when purchasing the toe-clamp binding. The beginner should get any toe-clamp (also called rattrap or racing, as well as Rottefella) binding which has metal nipples pointing upward from the plate and which has a clamp which is used to hold down the front part of the boot.

Price: From four to eight dollars.

Mounting the binding: The shop where the skis and binding are purchased will mount the binding on the skis. Instructions for mounting come with the binding. It is easy to do, but we recommend that the shop do this—mostly to make certain that the binding is installed precisely in regard to the skis' balancing point.

Heel plate: At the same time as the binding is being mounted, the skier should have a heel plate installed. It costs about one dollar. There are two kinds of heel plates. One is a square piece of metal having slightly raised edges and some rubber in the center. The other is simply a small piece of "V"-

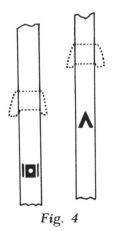

Fig. 4

shaped metal (*Fig. 4*). The heel plate goes directly under the heel of the boot. It serves two purposes: 1) to hold the heel steady on downhill running and turning (by friction); and 2) to stop the snow from bunching under the heel.

CABLE-AROUND-HEEL BINDING

This is a binding which is popular but which, in our opinion, is inferior to the toe-clamp binding. Some new skiers may have instructors who insist that they start out with a cable-around-heel type binding (also called Tempo or Jofa bindings; *Fig. 5*). We do

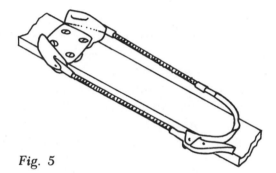

Fig. 5

not agree with this advice, but the instructor may have some special reason for prescribing this for certain individuals.

In the event that this happens, we are including information on Tempo and Jofa bindings as well as data on the special boots needed for them.

Type: 1) The Norwegian Tempo type—"Tempo" is a trade name and is sold everywhere, but any brand of this type is acceptable; or 2) the Swedish Jofa type, which is similar to the Norwegian Tempo type.

Description: There is a metal toe-cradle which holds the toe of the boot in place. A spring cable loops about the heel of the boot to hold the heel steady and, at the same time, to permit the heel to be raised and lowered easily.

The skier should make certain that there are adjustment screws in the bottom of the metal toe-cradle. This permits the binding to be adjusted to boot size. Some of these bindings are graduated into sizes: small, medium, and large. One should buy the boots before he gets the binding, and then should make certain that the binding fits the boot.

Price: About eight to fifteen dollars.

Mounting: The shop usually mounts the binding on the skis.

Heel plate: When buying the binding, a heel plate (which is a small piece of metal—either square with rubber in the center, or shaped like a "V") should also be purchased. It costs about one dollar. When the shop mounts the binding, the heel holder goes where the heel will rest on the ski. It serves two purposes: 1) to hold the heel steady on downhill runs (by friction); and 2) to stop the snow from bunching under the heel.

Boots

For the Toe-Clamp Binding

Type of boot: The general touring boot (*Fig. 6*).

Fig. 6

General characteristics: Light, flexible, soft leather, some padding, cut to *above* the anklebone.

Weight: Two or three pounds.

Sole: The sole is preferably leather. It extends in front of the toe and is square in shape in order to permit the metal toe-clamp to "clamp down" on it. (*Note:* Some boots have a composition sole which resembles rubber. This type of sole does not require metal eyelets into which the metal nipples can fit. The nipples simply push up into the soft sole. We recommend that the beginner get leather soles with metal eyelets in them or composition soles which have a metal plate with eyelets built into the composition. The new composition soles require less maintenance and don't wet through as quickly. Fitting the nipples into the exactly positioned eyelets guarantees getting the boot in precisely the right place.)

Fitting the nipples into the exactly positioned eyelets guarantees getting the boot in precisely the right place.)

Heel: The heel of the shoe designed for the toe clamp need *not* have a groove in it. If the shoe heel has a notch in it, it is designed for the cable-around-heel binding. There is no harm in having this type of shoe as long as the sole is made of smooth leather so that three metal eyelets can be installed under the toe area; but it often is a bit heavier and a little more expensive.

Type of leather: The skier should get the waterproof type.

Fitting the boot: The skier will wear two pairs of woolen socks in ski touring, so he should put on two pairs when trying on the boots. Almost all stores have "try on" socks available. The socks should *not* be tight. Loose socks allow good circulation and also allow perspiration to be evaporated or absorbed. The customer should put the boots on; he should then stand in them with the laces untied. It should be possible to move the foot backward and forward about a quarter of an inch to a half an inch. The heel should be kicked all the way back. The boots should now be laced. The skier should bend the knees and go forward to a kneeling position on the floor. The boots ought to be flexible enough to accomplish this easily with the forward part of the sole remaining flat on the floor. When kneeling, the toes should not be touching the front of the boots. If the boots are right, they will be the most comfortable shoes that the skier has ever worn; and he will have the inclination to wear them about the house instead of slippers.

Price: About twenty-five dollars.

FOR THE CABLE-AROUND-HEEL BINDING

The cable-around-heel binding requires a boot with a deep groove which goes around the back of the heel (*Fig. 7*). We

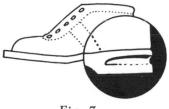

Fig. 7

suggest that he get one with either leather soles or composition which does not have deep serrations. This makes it easy to install metal eyelets should he later wish to switch to the toe-clamp binding.

Poles

The best poles for the beginner, in our opinion, are bamboo. Bamboo poles are cheaper, springier, and less fatiguing than fiberglass, aluminum, or steel poles.

Size: The poles should reach to just under the point where the arms join the outside of the shoulders (*Fig. 8*).

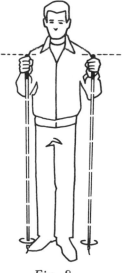

Fig. 8

Basket: The basket is a circular device near the bottom of the pole which prevents it from sinking into the snow more than a few inches (*Fig. 9*). It should not be more than 6 inches in diameter, and it should not have more than two cross-straps. Trial and error indicate that the 4½-inch diameter with two straps is the best combination over a great variety of snow conditions.

Fig. 9

Metal tip at the bottom of the pole: Cross-country ski poles have a pointed, curved metal tip at the bottom. If the tips are straight, they are not for cross-country work. The tip should be curved to assist in releasing the pole from the snow after the skier has moved forward.

Strap: At the top of the pole is a leather strap. We advise the skier buy the type of pole with the adjustable straps, even though they may be harder to find and may cost two or three dollars extra. After a bit of experience, he will wish to vary the size of the leather loop with different skiing conditions or temperatures (*Fig. 10*). Therefore, the skier should have the salesman demonstrate how to adjust the size of the strap loop, and should not leave the store until this has been learned. It is easy—simply a matter of pulling the leather thong in or out.

Fig. 10

Left and right pole: Not many skiers know it, but there is a left and a right pole (*Fig. 11*). The skier should have the salesman identify which is which, and should then put a mark, like a piece of tape, on the right pole so that it can be identified easily. If the poles are in the correct hands, the thumb will be resting on the underneath strap.

Price: From seven to twelve dollars.

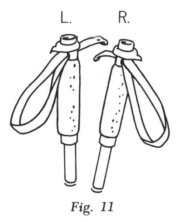

L.   R.

Fig. 11

Socks

Two pairs of socks are suggested in order to prevent the friction that comes with ski touring. Another reason for wearing two pairs is that the socks and the fairly loose boots form a layer of air which insulates the foot from the cold. The socks should not be tight (this is important!). Even if the socks are just a little tight, circulation *will be restricted* and perspiration will not evaporate; this will cause *cold* feet.

The inner pair should be good woolen socks. The outer can be ordinary athletic socks. The outer socks should be a size larger than the inner ones if the latter are of heavy wool. In the beginning, any length of sock is adequate; but after acquiring ski legs, many skiers enjoy wearing the traditional ski knickers—and for these, knee-length woolen socks are needed.

Price: Ankle-length woolen socks—about $2.50; knee-length woolen socks—from four to twelve dollars; athletic socks—about $1.25.

Beginner's Check-Off List for Cross-Country Waxes

WAX KIT

It is necessary to wax the bottoms of the skis before going out in the snow. The methods, the lessons, and the theory of waxing will be discussed in detail in Part IV, Chapters 24–27. The information given here concerns only what waxes to buy.

There are many brands of wax—ten that we know of—as follows: Swix (Norway and Sweden); Bratlie (Norway); Ex-Elit (Sweden); Haka (Finland); Holmenkol (Germany); Rex (Finland); Rode (Italy); Vauhti (Finland); Østbye (Norway); and Toko (Switzerland). They are all excellent. But we highly recommend that the skier choose one brand and stay with it until he becomes an expert. The choice should depend on which brand is most readily available. Swix and Rex are probably the most widely distributed in the United States. With the growing popularity of cross-country skiing, new waxes are appearing on the market; Ex-elit and Rode, for example, are now available in the United States.

Assuming that the skier starts with Swix or Rex, the following waxes should be bought when he gets his skiing equipment (waxes are identified by color): 1) *solid waxes*—one roll of green, one roll of blue, and one roll of purple (Swix) or violet (Rex); and 2) *fluid waxes* (these are called klisters and come in a tube)—red klister and blue klister (*Fig. 12*).

Fig. 12

There are other colors and types of wax. But for most snow conditions, especially the conditions easiest for the beginner, the above will suffice. Later, other waxes may be needed (see Chapter 26).

BASE PREPARATION MATERIAL

The bottom surface of the skis must be prepared in such a way as to seal out water and to provide a surface to which waxes will adhere. There are many base preparations but we recommend the tar compounds. If the shop where the skier buys his skis will prepare the ski base, we suggest that they use a "burn in" compound such as Holmenkol, Grundvalla (Rode), or Swix Wallco. Later, the skier will want to do this himself, and instructions will be given in Chapter 25.

For the beginner who wishes to prepare his own ski-bottom surfaces and who does not wish to use the "burn in" method which requires a heating torch of one sort or another, there are other compounds which can be applied quickly. These will sink into the wood without heat and will dry by air. These are

Østbye Aerosol, Rex Rapid Tar, Swix Special, Haka Rapid Tar, and Toko Grundvalla.

Although they are easier to apply, such bases do not last as long as the tars which are burned in, nor do they hold wax quite as well; but for the beginner they are adequate and will usually last a full season, with perhaps one or two touch-ups.

One can or tube of any of the above is enough to prepare a pair of skis; and instructions come with the product.

Our recommendation, however, is that the beginner have a tar compound burned in at the store.

Beginner's Check-Off List for Clothing

For the first few weeks the beginner has not yet learned how to "run and perspire" on skis and has not yet gone on long ski tours. Therefore, we suggest starting with the normal winter clothing—the looser and lighter, the better.

Long underwear (if it is cold enough to wear long underwear in normal outdoor activities). Later, when the skier moves quickly on long tours, we recommend fishnet underwear, since it does not hold much moisture next to the skin and dries quickly.

Ordinary out-of-door trousers (for both men and women).

The same amount of sweaters and parkas or jackets that are worn for ordinary outdoor activities (like ice skating or hiking).

Something to keep ears warm: Either a woolen earband, earmuffs, a hat which has ear flaps, or a parka which has a hood.

Gloves or mittens: We suggest mittens for beginners (later, the skier may prefer the less bulky gloves).

In short, beginners who live in colder climates do not have to buy any new clothes.

Once a beginner starts to get his ski legs, he will find, through experience, that in ski touring he will need less clothing than in other outdoor activities. He will be moving most of the time, and the body will generate much heat. When the beginner reaches the intermediate stage, he will wear much less clothing than he thought possible, and will still be warm. For instance, he will seldom wear gloves when the temperature is 25° F. and above.

If the beginner wishes to start off with the cross-country skier's special clothing, it is nice to know that it can be used for hiking, ice skating, and most of the other cold-weather outdoor activities (*Fig. 13*). It usually consists of knickers, long socks, and a parka with a hood. Knickers and parka cost about thirty-five to forty dollars. Knickers are loose and exceptionally functional.

Fig. 13

Note: Hardy beginners who can start off with little clothing should be certain to bring an extra sweater or parka when going out on the first tour (probably after about three lessons). This sweater should be tied around the waist or carried in a small rucksack. The reason for doing this is that the skier may wish to rest after a half an hour or more of tour and will need the extra sweater or parka to avoid getting chilled. *This is very important!*

A small rucksack (or day pack): This is not necessary, but it is a handy thing to have when touring. The skier may use it for carrying an extra sweater, extra gloves, wax, a Thermos of hot liquid, a camera, an emergency ski tip, etc. This is not needed by the beginner until after he starts on three- or four-hour tours. But a rucksack is handy to have, winter or summer.

Emergency ski tip: As soon as the skier starts going out on tours, he should carry an emergency ski tip. It is seldom needed, but if the ski tip breaks, the emergency tip is easily installed and makes getting back easier. The tips are made of aluminum and cost about two dollars each. Almost all ski stores sell them.

3

First Lesson on Skis

If possible, the first lesson should be taken under the easiest of conditions, which are as follows:

(1) *Location:* The first lesson can best be done on a front lawn, an open field, a golf course, a snow-covered playground, a nearby park, or the practice area at a ski resort. A half an acre is sufficient to get the feel of the skis and to acquire preliminary ski legs.

To practice on a lawn or field near home is advantageous for the beginner. It permits several short periods of ski learning in one day without travel; and it also allows one to have a family member or friend come out and read the lessons aloud to the beginner (*Fig. 1*). It will be of tremendous help to the beginner to have someone read the lessons aloud, step by step, and observe the beginner's ski positions and compare them to the diagrams in the book.

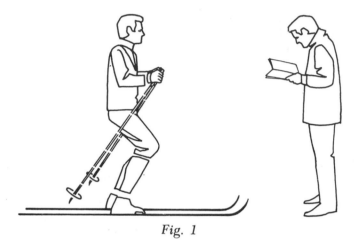

Fig. 1

Two people learning to cross-country ski together is even better. (Incidentally, cross-country touring is a sport which women and men learn with equal facility, and which adults can do with children.)

(2) *Temperature:* Preferably between 10° and 30° F. for the first few lessons. Waxing is simple in this temperature range; and it is easy to be physically comfortable during the slow exercise required at the beginning. See Chapter 26 for waxing.

(3) *Snow:* New-fallen snow or powder snow (or, snow which has been worked over and properly packed by professionals at the practice area of a ski resort) from 2 to 6 inches deep (over the already fallen base snow) is the easiest to ski on. If the new snow is deeper than about 6 inches, the skier should put the skis on and should take tiny side steps for the hundred-foot-long practice area needed; or walk over it with snowshoes. This pats snow down.

Conditions to avoid, if possible, when starting:

(1) One should avoid extremely cold, windy, unpleasant

weather. Later, when the skier has had more experience and has learned to move quickly, he won't mind the cold.

(2) One should avoid temperatures over 30° F. because it will complicate the waxing problem. (After a few lessons, this will no longer be a problem.)

(3) One should avoid crusty, icy, or slushy snow at the beginning.

(4) One should avoid deep, soft snow which buries the skis. (Such conditions can be made satisfactory by side stepping on skis or by using snowshoes to stamp the soft snow down.)

(5) One should avoid terrain with abrupt slopes close to the practice area.

We now have good temperature, good snow, and a good location. The skier should wax the skis, as shown in Chapter 27. Now let us go outside and learn to ski. (But one mustn't forget to put the skis outside first—for at least ten minutes—to let the wax cool. If this is not done, the bottoms may ice up and stick to the snow, making movement difficult.)

The skis should be put flat on the snow, parallel to one another, about a foot apart. Although the skis are identical now, after the binding is attached to them there will be a left ski and a right ski (*Fig. 2*). It is easy to tell which is the right ski and which is the left. The part of the binding which flares out is always on the outside (a fact which is true for all types of binding). The lever which tightens the heel cable in the Tempo-type binding must always be on the outside.

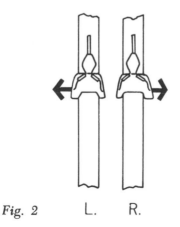

Fig. 2   L.   R.

The poles should be placed upright in the snow within reaching distance, one on each side of the skis. The skier should brush the snow from the soles of the boots and the ski binding. If bending over is difficult, he can hold on to the poles for balance.

If the toe-clamp-type binding is used:

(1) The skier should brush the snow from the soles of the boots and from the ski binding.

(2) With the movable clamp in a vertical position, the boot is pushed into the binding. When the boot is moved all the way forward, the metal pegs which come up from the binding (usually there are three of them) will fit into the eyelets recessed into the sole of the boot (*Fig. 3*).

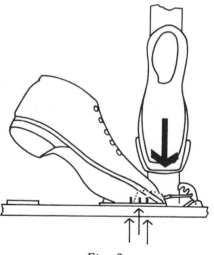

Fig. 3

(3) The foot should be gently jiggled back and forth to make certain that the metal pegs are seated in the eyelets. If the pegs are not firmly set in the metal eyelets, they will chew holes in the sole of the boot.

(4) The movable clamp is now pushed forward and hooked

into the curved metal piece which is mounted on the ski a few inches in front of the toe piece.

If the Tempo-type binding is used:

(1) The skier should step into the binding of one ski by slipping the toe of the boot into the toe piece of the binding.

(2) He must make certain that the square leather extension of the boot sole is all the way under the metal hold-down "clips" of the binding (*Fig. 4*).

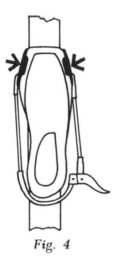

Fig. 4

(3) He must also make sure that both the toe and heel are centered on the ski. If the boot is at an angle to the ski, the ski may be on the wrong foot.

(4) The heel cable is slipped around the back of the boot and placed in the groove which is in the heel of the boot. (If the boot has no cable groove, the rear of the cable should be placed at the point where the heel joins the main part of the boot. This will work adequately provided the cable has been fitted properly at the time the boots, binding, and skis were purchased.)

(5) The lever which tightens the cable is now pulled back. If the cable is of the right length, it will take a considerable

amount of pressure to pull the cable-tightening lever (*Fig.* 5). (*Note:* The cable should have been properly adjusted at the ski shop. However, if this has not been done, it is simple to tighten or loosen it as needed by screwing the cable into or out of the threaded receptacle at the end.)

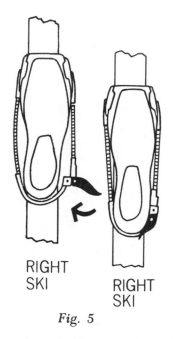

RIGHT
SKI
                    RIGHT
                    SKI

Fig. 5

The skis are now attached to the skier and the first skiing lesson can begin. *Some of the first exercises may appear absurdly simple, and the impatient beginner may be inclined to skip them. We urge the beginner not to do so. A few days spent in acquiring the basic positions and movements of cross-country skiing will greatly speed up the process of becoming an expert. It will avoid having to unlearn bad ski habits later.*

Rudimentary Ski Movements (and Getting the Feel of the Skis)

(1) The poles are grasped as shown (*Fig 6*). They are placed in the snow at each side of each ski, about a foot away from the heels of the boots.

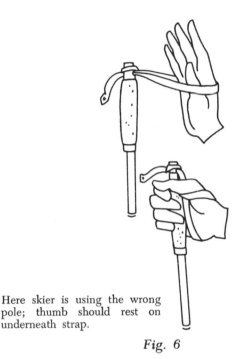

Here skier is using the wrong pole; thumb should rest on underneath strap.

Fig. 6

(2) The feet are flexed, first one and then the other, just to convince the skier how comfortable and maneuverable cross-country equipment is.

(3) The skier now goes into a half-sitting position. The feet should be flat (the skier should carefully check Figure 7 at this point). To get into this position, the knees should be bent exactly as if starting to sit down in a chair, *but keep the back*

straight and vertical. The skier must *keep his head up!* At first, it will be necessary to support some of the body weight on the poles. (*Note:* This is not a *full* sitting position; it is a slight sitting position—one which people seventy or eighty years old can hold with ease.)

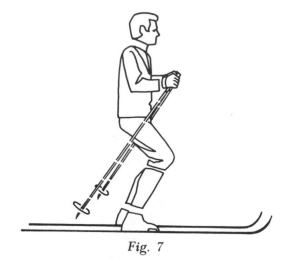

Fig. 7

The amount of the "sitting down" should be varied by moving up and down, noting all the while how the poles carry more weight as the crouch increases, and less as it decreases.

(4) While remaining in one place (but still half sitting), the skier should slide one ski forward and backward about 18 inches in a shuffling movement, *keeping the ski on the snow.* The other ski is now shuffled in the same way.

(5) Still in the half-sitting position, the skier lifts one ski 6 inches above the snow and then puts it down.

Then the other ski is lifted several inches off the ground and is put down.

All of the above (steps 1 through 5) are repeated, alternating the skis as if walking in place.

While doing these exercises, one should notice how easily and automatically *even the beginner* shifts his weight from one ski to the other, how easily the poles support the weight of the body when needed, and how the poles help the skier maintain his balance. The interaction of poles, skis, legs, and body is natural, because cross-country skiing is almost as natural as walking. The half sitting plus the natural, relaxed interactions are the keys to cross-country skiing.

(6) The skier now stands up straight and places the skis about a foot apart from one another.

The poles are placed about 8 inches to the side of each ski and about 2 feet in front of the boots.

The skier should lean forward slightly, without moving the skis, in order to get the feeling of supporting part of the body weight on the poles while the body is at an angle (*Fig.* 8).

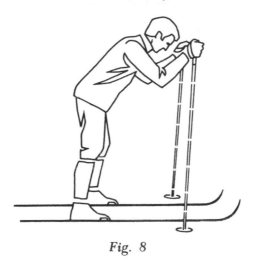

Fig. 8

(7) Still leaning forward, the skier slides one foot forward and backward; then the other. *The ski should not be lifted from the snow while doing this.*

(8) The skier now stands up straight and moves the poles back so that they are about a foot from the sides of the skis and just a few inches from the heel of the boot. From this position he will learn how to do a simple step turn.

The Step Turn

This simple turn is learned while standing in place. It is easy. The same movements will later be used to make turns while running down narrow trials or while gliding down open slopes.

The step turn to the left:

(1) The skier assumes the half-sitting position described above (*Fig. 7*), using the poles for balance and support.

(2) The left ski is moved *forward* until the left boot-toe is a few inches ahead of the right boot-toe.

(3) The tip of the left ski is lifted about a foot off the ground. The tail of the ski will lightly touch the snow. The ski is at an angle, with the tip up and the tail in the snow (*Fig. 9*). If there is any difficulty, it is because the toe of the raised ski is not far enough ahead of the other ski.

Fig. 9

(4) The left ski is moved slightly to the left in a circular motion (beginners are most comfortable swinging the ski through about a 30° arc). The ski is placed flat on the snow, and the skier's weight is put on it.

(5) The right ski is brought around in the same way, until it is parallel to the left ski.

(6) The poles are moved into relatively the same position as at the start, and the step turn is repeated until the skier is facing in the desired direction. Figure 10 shows what the ski tracks look like.

Fig. 10

(7) The skier now repeats all the steps, but this time going to the right.

That's all there is to it. We will now learn how to move ahead over the snow and cover distance.

Moving Ahead over Snow and Covering Distance

(1) The poles are placed about a foot to the side of each ski, opposite the boot.

(2) The skier should drop into the half-sitting position, keeping his head up.

(3) Still half sitting, he now shuffles forward, starting with steps of about a foot in length. While shuffling forward, he should use the pole in a way which provides the most balance. The correct pole technique will be described later, but chances are that the beginner is using his pole correctly.

(4) The skier should move ahead about a hundred feet.

Using the step turn, he turns around and comes back in the same track. It is desirable to practice shuffling forward and step turning for about ten minutes, back and forth, back and forth, alternating the step turns, first to the left and then to the right.

(5) The poles are then discarded and this exercise is repeated for ten minutes.

When the above exercises are satisfactorily completed, a considerable feeling of security on the skis will be apparent. It is now possible for the beginner to enjoy short tours on flat terrain. Exploring and experimenting may now begin. The skier may go for perhaps twenty minutes across meadows, a golf course, a park, or an open field—any flat area. But he should not as yet attempt to go down slopes. That he may do after learning the second lesson.

The beginner is now familiar with:

(1) The half-sitting position (always holding the head up).

(2) The forward shuffle.

(3) The step turn.

In one hour the beginner has learned three of the basic positions and movements of cross-country skiing.

In the next lesson, he will learn how to go downhill.

4

Straight Downhill Running on Cross-Country Skis

Cross-country skiing not only provides the pleasure of being able to ski downhill, but also of being able to go fairly fast along the flats as well as at a surprising speed uphill. Wherever a person can walk, uphill or down, he can go on cross-country skis. (This is in contrast to the alpine skier—the breed most known and publicized in America—who must be towed uphill by mechanical equipment, and who can go only short distances on the flats without fatigue and pain caused by his "Iron Maiden" boots.

How to go downhill: The skier should pick a gentle slope— one which is from 50- to 200-feet long and in which the difference in elevation between top and bottom is from 15 to 20 feet.

A slope should be chosen which has a "run out" at the bottom. A "run out" indicates that the terrain has a natural means of allowing the skier to coast to a stop when he is at the bottom of his downhill run—either a flat area or a slight uphill slope at the bottom of the hill (*Fig. 1*).

Fig. 1

The reason for having a run out: During the first few downhill runs, the beginner should not have to worry about whether or not he will be able to stop. He needs an 'area where he can stop at the bottom without effort.

The snow conditions and temperature should preferably be the same as described for the first lesson. If it has snowed overnight, it is a simple matter for the beginner to pack down the snow if it is more than 4 to 6 inches deep. He can do this by taking small sideway steps with the skis, going slowly up the slope. In this fashion he will pack down an area which is as wide as the ski is long. (See pages 86–89 for a lesson in how to side step up steep hills).

The beginners' slope at most ski resorts will also provide an excellent learning area. Here, the packing down of the snow usually has been done by experts with equipment designed for that purpose.

How to start downhill running: The skier should go to the top of the slope, put on his skis, and take a stance in which his feet are about a foot apart. Standing in place, he should shuffle the skis back and forth (one ski at a time) ten or twelve times.

This provides a feel for the snow and also removes any snow which may have stuck to the bottom of the skis. If the skier starts downhill with balled-up snow under his skis, the skis will stick and cause him to push backward with his poles or try to jerk the stuck skis loose. As a result, the skier may lose his balance.

After shuffling the skis on the snow, the skier drops down into the half-sitting position. This is the same position that was practiced in Chapter 3. The knees are bent, thus lowering the buttocks about 6 or 8 inches.

The skier must keep his head up and look forward. This greatly assists in maintaining the correct half-sitting position.

If the half-sitting position is executed correctly, the skier's feet will be flat on his skis. *The weight of his body will be distributed evenly between the ball and the heel of the foot* (Fig. 2). The skier now shifts the body weight forward and backward a few inches, finding the exact position in which this weight may be evenly distributed on the feet. When this even distribution of weight occurs, the skier will experience a comfortable feeling which is known as "the balanced position."

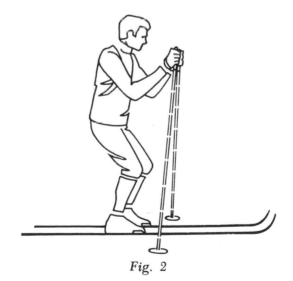

Fig. 2

The skier is now almost ready to go down the slope.

He should take a look down the slope to make certain that there are no people or *obstacles* ahead.

He should be in the balanced position, drop the hands to thigh level, hold the pole shafts back and keep the baskets off the snow, and shuffle until the glide down begins (*Fig.* 3).

Fig. 3

When he is on the slope, he will begin to glide slowly downhill. The first time down may seem awkward because it is a new experience, and the skier may even lose his balance and fall a few times. No harm. It is almost impossible to get hurt; and with cross-country equipment, it is easy to get up. If at any time during the run the skier feels extremely uneasy, he may recover security by moving his skis further apart—to shoulder width at least.

The skier glides to the bottom of the slope until he comes to a natural stop.

He then step-turns around and goes back up the slope. The incline of the practice hill will be so slight that getting back up should be no problem. If, at this stage, the skier cannot get back up the slope, then the slope is too steep for practice.

The skier should go to the top of slope and repeat the lesson.

He must practice going downhill until he finally acquires a small measure of confidence. Two small, additional techniques should be learned:

(1) Instead of shuffling off the top of the slope, one should push off with the poles. When the slide downhill starts, the poles are held backward, but with tips off the snow (*Fig. 4*).

(2) As the movement down the slope begins, one ski tip is pushed about 8 inches in front of the other. It makes no difference which ski is ahead.

One ski is kept about 8 inches ahead of the other all the way down the slope (*Fig. 4*).

Fig. 4

The reason for having one ski tip slightly ahead of the other is to provide fore and aft balance. This helps the skier maintain the balanced position even if he should go over a change in surface, like a bump or uneven terrain such as an unseen snowdrift.

The skier continues this straight downhill running for at least a half an hour. During this practice, he alternates putting first one ski tip ahead and then the other. After a few downhill runs, the skier will learn which is his natural "ahead" ski.

During these easy, straight downhill runs, the beginner will soon learn that it is almost impossible to get hurt. If he loses his balance and falls a few times, he will find that it is rather fun toppling over occasionally, and that it is easy to get up.

He will discover that, after about ten runs down the gentle slope, he has become naturally relaxed and can experience noticeable progress even within as short a time period as an hour.

We have never yet had a student who, by the end of this lesson, did not have an urge to begin skiing up and down steeper and steeper hills. This is how it should be. But before he can go to the steep hills, he should learn 1) how to slow his speed if necessary and 2) how to control and change the direction in which he is skiing.

In the next chapter, we will discuss "snowplowing," which is one of the ways of slowing downhill speed.

Hint: In learning to "crouch," most beginners make the mistake of dropping their hands too low, thus their poles are almost parallel to the snow and are of little help in keeping balance. Do not let hands drop beneath eye level when crouching.

5

Controlling Speed by Snowplowing

In this lesson, the same gentle slope that was used in the previous lessons is used here. The skier will now learn how to slow down his speed when skiing downhill. One of the methods used to achieve this is "snowplowing." In a later lesson, another method will be taught.

Snowplowing means just what the term indicates. While coming downhill, the skier slows down by plowing the snow with his skis.

The skis are moved into an upside-down "V" position, or the plow position (as seen from the skier's vantage point), with the tips of the skis coming together to form the base of the "V" (or the forward part of the plow) and with the heels of the skis spread apart (*Fig. 1*).

Note: Although the skis are like a plow, the tips do not touch. They should be about 6 inches apart.

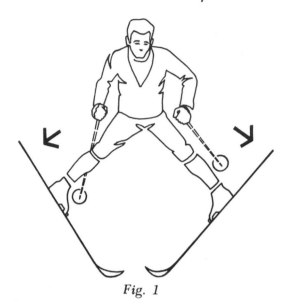

Fig. 1

Here is how the snowplow is done:

(1) After the skier has begun to move down the practice slope, he should force the tails of the skis outward. The tips of the skis stay in about the same position. *It is the tails which move outward to form the "V."*

The tails may be moved outward by keeping the feet flat on the skis and pressing down hard on the heels. The knees should be bent more than they are for the "half sit" and should then be pressed together, forcing the tails of the skis outward.

While doing this, the eyes are kept on the tips of the skis to make certain that they stay in the original position and do not cross. They will not cross if the skier concentrates on forcing the tails out.

The skis are now in the "V" position. The next move is to rotate the skis at an angle so that the edges will dig into the snow and begin to plow.

This is done by rolling the ankles inward. The skis then will dig in (*Fig. 2*).

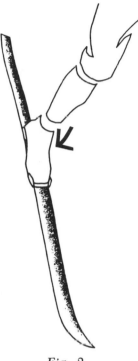

Fig. 2

When the skier is in this snowplow position, he will slow down.

There are many instances when the snowplow should not be used: for example, when going down at high speeds or in deep snow. This will be discussed later.

The skier should spend about a half an hour going down the easy slope, stopping or slowing down by using the snowplow.

For a forceful snowplow, the tails of the skis should be 4 or 5 feet apart (the open part of the "V"). The skier will frequently only have them about 2 feet apart and not realize it. At the end of the trip down the hill, he should look back at the tracks left in the snow. Not only will the tracks indicate if the ski tails have been spread far enough apart, but will also show if one ski has been pushed out more than the other.

When the skier reaches the end of his run and is turning to go uphill again, he must *be certain to make the step turns carefully*. He should concentrate on them, and especially on lifting the tip of the ski while keeping its tail on the snow. In a few lessons the skier will learn how to do this while going downhill. The more precisely he does it on the flats, the easier it will be while moving downhill.

But, first, we will show the skier how to turn by using the half plow, a variation of the position he has just been practicing. This will be the aim of the next chapter.

6

The Half-Plow Turn

The skier now knows how to ski down gentle slopes straight. He also knows one way in which to slow himself when skiing downhill at slow speed (i.e., with the snowplow).

The next thing he must learn is how to make turns while going downhill. This makes possible the fun of skiing down steep hills and along winding trails.

Turning is not only a method of changing direction but is also a technique for slowing down if going too fast. (*Note:* The snowplow generally should not be used for slowing down at high speeds where there is deep snow or rough terrain. An unexpected and unseen snowdrift may catch the ski tips and send the skier tumbling.)

On open hills, it is better to slow down by using other methods. One of them is by turning—that is, by changing direction from straight downhill to across the hill or even uphill. By doing this, the angle of descent is reduced; hence, the speed is reduced. By turning parallel to the side of the hill, the skier can eliminate the angle of descent and reduce his speed further or stop. Or, the skier may turn up into the hill—thus surely stopping (*Fig. 1*).

Fall Line: the path a ball would take if it rolled downhill naturally.

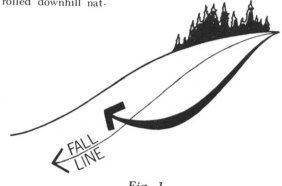

Fig. 1

There are two basic methods of turning while skiing downhill on cross-country skis: 1) the half snowplow; and 2) the step turn. (There is a third method—the parallel turn—which can be executed to near perfection by only a few professionals; but cross-country bindings make this turn extremely difficult to do.)

Beginners should first learn the half-snowplow (or the half-plow) turn. The following lesson concerns this technique.

The Half-Plow Turn

(1) The skier should begin by skiing straight down the slope.

(2) He should then go into the snowplow position.

(3) To turn to the left, the skier should simply put most of

the body weight on the right ski. He then should simultaneously angle the inside edge of the ski into the snow. This is the
same kind of edging as is done in the full snowplow. Naturally,
the weighted ski will carry the skier in the direction in which
the ski is pointed. In this instance, the right ski has all the
body weight on it and is pointing about 45° to the left (*Fig. 2*).
The skier will almost immediately (and with little physical
strain) turn to the left. *Important: Once the ski is weighted,
the skier should hold the downhill shoulder slightly back.*

Fig. 2

(4) As the turn starts, the skier should slide the left ski
around so that it is parallel to the right ski and is pointing in
the new direction. *Note: The left ski should not be lifted from
the snow.*

A simple turn to the left has now been completed.

(5) The skier is no longer going straight down the slope. He
now is traversing the hill to the left at an angle of 45°. He
should continue to keep most of the body weight on the right

ski after having made the left turn, *because the right ski is now the downhill ski.*

Note: When diagonally crossing a hill, there will always be an uphill ski and a downhill ski. *One should always keep most of the body weight on the downhill ski.* It is like standing sideways on a flight of stairs. The weight will be on the foot which is on the lower step.

(6) After making the turn to the left (with the skis now moved so that they are parallel to one another, the skier should continue to the bottom of the gentle slope and stop.

(7) The skier should then return to the top of the slope and, once again, should start skiing straight downhill. He must go into a full snowplow; and from that position should put the weight on the left foot, and turn to the right while *keeping the downhill shoulder slightly back.* The skier should now bring the right ski parallel to the left and continue down the easy slope. He will be traversing the slope, *and must keep the weight on the downhill ski.* In this case (turning to the right), the downhill ski will be the left one.

(8) This exercise should be repeated a dozen times, alternating between turning left and turning right.

(9) The exercise should then be repeated six more times, but now without poles. The poles should be left at the top of the hill.

(10) After these exercises have been completed, the skier places one of the poles halfway down the slope. Coming straight down the slope, he should aim for a spot about 10 feet to the side of the pole. When approaching the pole, the skier should do a half plow so as to turn as close to the pole as possible (*Fig. 3*).

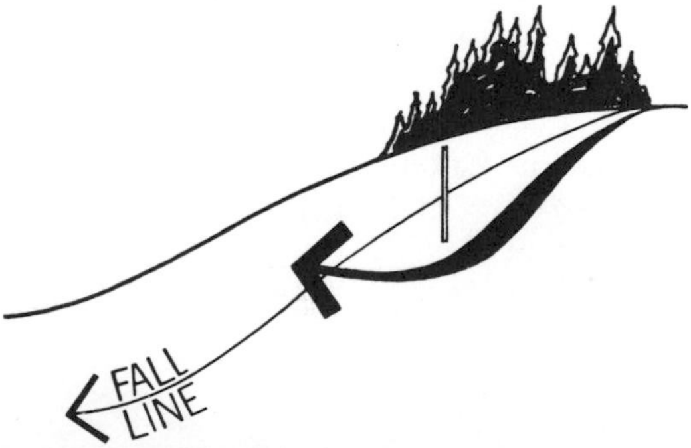

Fig. 3

(11) The skier must then go back up the hill and repeat the exercise, but this time passing the pole on the other side.

(12) After doing this, the second pole should be placed about 50 feet below the first pole. Now, coming straight down the slope, the skier should make a turn at the first pole. As soon as the skis are parallel, he should go into the snowplow position again and turn in the opposite direction past the second pole (*Fig. 4*).

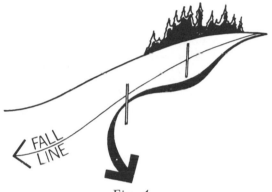

Fig. 4

After a few tries, the skier will be able to judge the speed of his turn (remembering all the while that this still is on a gentle slope and that, therefore, the speed of turn will be slow). It is important that the skier learn these linked half-plow turns; that is, going first in one direction and then the other (*Fig. 5*).

Fig. 5

For the remainder of the lesson, the skier should "fool around" and experiment. But no matter how confident and cocky he is (and he will be!), we urge him to remain on the gentle slopes—to stay off the steeper hills until he learns how to go *up* steep ones (Chapter 10).

But one should not be afraid to experiment! The novice should, by all means, go on a short tour, among gently rolling hills if possible, starting off straight down, then turning and gliding the rest of the way across the hill (traversing). The directions should be varied, and the skier should sometimes use his poles and sometimes not. He should practice turning halfway around poles which have been placed at varying intervals down the hill. Naturally, the closer the poles, the more abrupt the second turn will have to be.

Now that the beginner has gotten the feel of the half-plow turn, he is ready to learn the step turn, which is the most frequently used turn and the one that he will use at higher speeds and on winding trails. For this, we must proceed to the next chapter.

7

The Moving Step-Turn

The moving step-turn is one of the most frequently used techniques in cross-country skiing; and one of the most satisfying. It is used for turning while going downhill and also while moving ahead on the flats.

First, we will discuss how the step turn is used while going downhill.

The beginner should go back to Chapter 3, "First Lesson on Skis," and should reread how the step turn was done while standing in one place (rather than while skiing). Step turning while moving downhill utilizes basically the same technique.

The skier should start skiing down the practice slope. It is essential that he crouch and *press down on his heels*, acquiring in this way a flat-footed stance on the skis. If this position is remembered, the skier will have no trouble with the downhill step-turn. He now starts to go straight down the slope. After the forward motion has begun, one small step to the right should be taken, exactly as is done on the flats save one exception—the left pole is used to help push the skier to the right. It is a gentle push—almost more to sustain balance than to swing the skier around.

After having taken this one step to the right, the left ski is brought around so that it is parallel to the right ski. The skier should continue moving down the slope.

He is now moving downhill, but is veering slightly to the right. As soon as he feels comfortably balanced, another step to the right is taken. This should be repeated once more before reaching the bottom.

By now the skier is probably at the bottom of the practice slope.

The skier now returns to the top of the slope.

He starts down again. As soon as there is forward motion, the same procedure is followed; but instead of taking one step to the right, several small steps are taken, one after the other (*Fig. 1*).

Fig. 1

Then, returning again to the top of the slope, the exercises are repeated, only this time turning to the left on the way down.

What makes the step turn so easy to execute when going downhill is the crouching position of the skier coupled with the pressure placed on the skier's heels. In all the downhill parts of cross-country skiing, the skier should always be crouching and pressing down on his heels; he will, then, always be ready to make a quick turn.

The skier should go down the slope again. After the forward propulsion starts, he should take two small steps to the left. When this has been completed, two small steps to the right should be taken.

The skier is now heading straight down the slope. Two more small steps to the right are taken; then, two more to the left.

The novice should go down the practice slope over and over again, alternating directions by going first to the left and then to the right.

On the first day of learning the step turn, we suggest that the skier not take more than three steps at a time and that he keep them very small.

On the second day of practicing the step turn, the skier, after starting down the slope, should take as many steps to the left as is necessary to turn up into the hill enough to prevent forward motion.

This should be practiced going to the left and then to the right.

When this has been done, two sticks (not the ski poles—they are needed for the step turn) should be placed about 40 feet apart on the ski slope so that the skier may practice turning around them in opposite directions (*Fig. 2*).

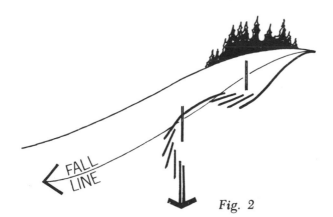

Fig. 2

Hints: When going down fast trails, the inclination of the skier is to start turning too late. This happens simply because he does not take his forward motion into consideration. Novices should begin the step turn by as much as 10 feet sooner than they believe they should. Of course, the faster one is traveling, the sooner the step turn must be started. After a little practice, the timing will start to come naturally, without thinking.

If the skier has problems with balance, he can get the feeling of proper weight shifting with the following exercise. A one-step step turn should be made, say to the left. As soon as the skier has stepped off to the left, all of the weight will be on the left ski (*Figs. 3 and 4*). It should be kept on the one ski as the skier continues down the hill. After going 5 or 6 feet, the weight which is put on the two skis should be equalized. Then another step turn to the left should be taken and the procedure repeated. After this has been completed, the skier should go through the same thing again, but this time turning to the right. After having done this several times, he should go back to the top of the slope and try normal step turning, taking two or three steps in the regular manner. It should now be easier to maintain the proper balance.

Figs. 3 and 4

One ought not to forget that a slight push on the "outside" pole helps the skier make his turn.

Step turning while moving on the flats is done in exactly the same way as in downhill skiing. The difference is that the skier is usually moving more slowly on the flats than on hills.

With increased practice and experience, the skier will develop a lead-in to the step turn on the flats as well as a follow-through, with double-pole motion. This is an important technique for increased smoothness and speed. A series of step turns with the double-pole motion should be practiced. Double poling means pushing ahead with both poles. The fine points of this technique are explained on page 107. It is important to practice this with a series of step turns. Do one. A few seconds later do another. Vary direction. Do several to the left, then several to the right; then alternate left and right. To start, practice the step turns on a wide, gentle hill. If the speed downhill seems too much for the beginner, make two or three step turns in the same direction. This will bring the skier parallel to the hill. He will no longer be going downhill, and the speed will diminish.

Notes: Be certain to bear down on your heels so that the tail of the ski never leaves the snow surface; as the ski is moved through an angle in the desired direction, the tip (the front) —*but not the heel*—is lifted about 6 inches.

When an expert goes down a fast, curving trail, he makes his quick step turns with a series of rapid hippity-hops in the direction he wants to go. When watching an old master like Herman Johannsen (still skiing at 97), one understands how he got his nickname, "Jack Rabbit."

8

Getting Up After a Fall

Like alpine skiers, cross-country skiers frequently fall when they are learning how to ski down hills. It is, however, almost impossible to get hurt under the conditions in which beginners are learning. Surprisingly enough, most falls result in laughter, not complaints. However, since a skier is bound to fall, he should learn how to get up easily.

We suggest that the skier practice both falling and getting up.

He should go to a very slight slope and side-step up the side 5 or 10 feet; then, by simply relaxing (or call it "collapsing on purpose"), the skier should fall down onto the snow either by

going backward, sideways, or straight down on the buttocks
(*Figs. 1 and 2*). Sideways may be the most natural.

Figs. 1 and 2

Getting up from a fall is easy.

(1) The pole straps should be removed from the wrists.

(2) While the skier is lying on his side, the skis should be
brought around so that they are parallel to one another. This is
usually easy; but if necessary, the skier should roll onto his

Fig. 3

back so that both skis are in the air over his body (*Fig.* 3). He should then swing them so that they are parallel to one another and across the slope below and should lower them into the snow, at right angles to the fall line.

(3) If there is snow in the skier's gloves, around the wrists, under the collar, or around the waist, now is a good time to shake it off or brush it out.

(4) The knees should be bent so that the skis are brought under the body as close as possible.

(5) The edges of the skis should be dug into the snow.

(6) The skier should grasp both poles so that they are next to each other, thus acting as a single pole (*Fig. 4*).

Fig. 4

The points are placed uphill about a foot from the knees.
The poles are grasped just above the baskets with one hand, and the other hand is placed halfway up the shafts.

The skier can now push himself up into a sitting position *or onto his knees,* and then up into the standing position (*Fig. 5*).

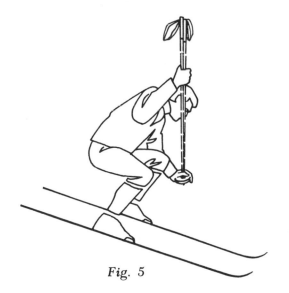

Fig. 5

If on a slope, it is important for the skis to be parallel to the side of the hill. If the skis are not parallel to the side of the hill, they will slide downhill as the skier gets up (*Fig. 6*). Nothing is more frustrating or tiring than getting a part of the

WRONG WAY

Fig. 6

way up and then beginning to slide downhill out of control. This usually results in another fall.

9

The Kick Turn

While standing on the side of a hill, the kick turn is the *only* safe way of turning completely around. On the flats, it is the quickest method of reversing direction. *The step turn, which the skier learned earlier, will not do for turning completely around when standing on a hill* because the skier will tend to slide down the hill, either forward or backward, in the middle of his turn.

The kick turn should first be learned on flat ground.

The Kick-Turn on Flat Terrain

The first turn will be to the right.

Standing on the skis on flat ground with the poles in normal

position, one on each side just in front of the boots, the skier
should shift most of the body weight to the left ski and move
the left pole further to the left. Although most of the weight is
on the left ski, the poles are supporting a little of the weight in
order to help maintain balance.

The skier should now lift the right foot straight forward and
up so that the ski is at a 45° angle to the ground. The tail of
the right ski will have slid forward so that it is halfway between the left foot and the tip of the left ski (*Fig. 1*).

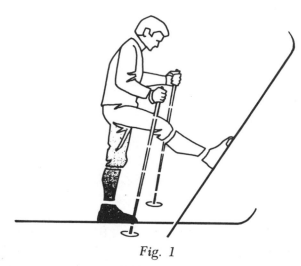

Fig. 1

The skier should rotate his body 90° to the right while simultaneously moving the right pole around to the right so that
it is behind the body (and is on the same side that the left pole
is on; *Fig. 2*). But, he should make sure that the right pole is
placed *beyond* the tail of the left ski. This is done in order to
stop the left ski from hitting the right pole during a later
move.

Fig. 2

At this stage, everything except the left foot and left ski has been swung around to the right.

This position should be held for a moment, so that the skier can feel comfortable. He can easily maintain his balance because he now has four points of contact with the earth: the entire left ski, the tail of the right ski, and both poles.

After standing motionless for a moment, the right ski is swung around another 90° to the right and is placed flat on the snow. During this movement, the tail of the right ski will remain in approximately the same place. The only motion of the right ski has been a circular one and, later, one of placing it flat on the ground.

The left ski is still pointing in its original direction; the right ski is pointing in the opposite direction (*Fig. 3*). (To feel comfortable, the knees should be bent forward.)

Fig. 3

Since both skis are flat on the snow and are pointing in opposite directions and since both feet are flat on their skis, then
there must be an accompanying shift in the distribution of the
body weight so that it is now evenly divided between the left
foot and the right (not forgetting that small amount of weight
still on both poles).

Both of the poles are held behind the body.

The left pole is now removed from the snow. The skier will
still find it easy to maintain his balance because he has three
points of contact with the ground: the two skis and the right
pole.

The body weight should be shifted so that almost all of it is
on the right ski.

The left ski is lifted a few inches from the snow, and the left
leg and left ski are swung around and rotated 180° to the
right (Fig. 4). The left ski is then placed on the snow so that it
is parallel to the right ski.

Fig. 4

The left pole is simultaneously swung around and placed on the left side of the left ski.

The kick turn to the right has now been completed.

The turn should be executed five more times to the right. Then five times to the left. And once more to the right; and then once more to the left.

By now the skier will feel comfortable and secure in making the kick turn on flat terrain. Very little difficulty should be experienced if the skier practices.

The Kick Turn on the Hill

The skier must now go about 10 feet up a gentle slope (later, he can do this on very steep hills).

He should stand sideways to the hill so that the skis are horizontal to it—that is, forming a right angle with an imaginary line going straight down the hill (i.e., the "fall line"). Because the skis are horizontal to the hill, the skier will not slide backward or forward.

The kick turn on the hill, with one exception, is done exactly as it is done on the flats.

The one exception involves the taking of precautions to stop the skis from sliding sideways down the hill while the turn is being executed.

Sliding sideways down the hill is prevented by digging the uphill edges of the skis into the snow.

During the entire turn, whichever ski is on the snow must have its uphill side edged into it (*Fig. 5*).

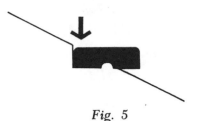

Fig. 5

We will repeat: the kick turn should be done on the hill exactly as it is done on the flats, but the skier should make absolutely certain that 1) the skis are horizontal to the hill before starting the turn (this is to stop the skier from sliding forward or backward down the slope); and 2) the uphill edges of the skis are always edged into the snow (this is to stop the skier from slipping sideways down the slope).

Having mastered this, the skier is ready to learn how to ski uphill.

10

Uphill

One of the most joyful aspects of cross-country skiing is being able to ski uphill.

The cross-country skier needs no mechanical equipment. Using only his skis and his legs, he can go where he wants. He can climb uphill as fast as he could run up the same slope in summer.

The keys to this marvel are 1) the wax on the bottom of the ski; and 2) the uphill techniques which we will describe here.

The fundamentals of uphill climbing are simple. But we urge the skier to learn them slowly and well.

Being able to ski uphill makes it possible to explore miles of countryside, to follow old logging roads, bridle paths, and semicleared sections of sparsely inhabited areas (and such spots can be found close at hand, even in New York City).

There are five uphill techniques: 1) straight uphill climbing (the one used most often, and the fastest); 2) the uphill traverse; 3) the side step; 4) the herringbone; and 5) the traverse side step. Each will be explained.

The method chosen usually depends upon the steepness of the hill, the type of snow, and the width of the trail. (A trail is a path, cleared of trees and bushes. Usually it is from about 3 to 10 feet wide.) Once the skier has mastered the five techniques, he will almost instinctively know which to use. Naturally, he will start with the fastest; if this doesn't work, he will switch to a slower but surer method.

When starting the uphill-climbing lessons, we urge the skier to continue, if possible, with the ideal skiing conditions described in the first lesson. Such conditions not only make skiing easier, but they simplify the waxing problem. Under these conditions, the skier can work with either blue or green hard wax. If the skier starts with green wax and finds himself slipping, he should put some blue right over it. If conditions are not ideal and the skier is eager to practice, then we refer him to Chapter 25 for more advanced waxing techniques.

Climbing Straight Uphill

The key to climbing is to make the ski hold firmly in the snow without slipping backward. When pressure is properly applied to the ski, the wax on the bottom of the ski will press against the snow crystals and grip them sufficiently to prevent the ski from sliding.

The position of the body is important. The beginner should look at the illustration before going any further.

The skier must "sit" lower than he does when skiing on the flats. The knees must be bent more. Actually, the body is only about 3 inches lower than the normal crouch which is used when coming downhill; but to the beginner it feels like much more (*Fig. 1*).

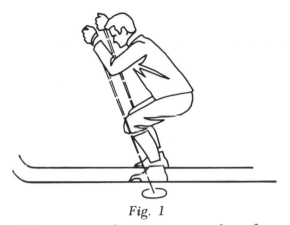

Fig. 1

There will be an initial temptation to lean forward (*Fig. 2*).
This is wrong.

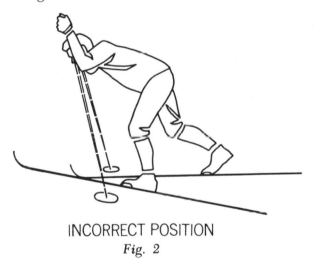

INCORRECT POSITION
Fig. 2

The skier must not lean forward—just sit down more. When
going uphill, the beginner will have the feeling that he is leaning backward; but he is not—he is merely lower. (To get a
feeling for this, the "uphill" position can be practiced at home
without putting on skis. The skier should go into the half-sitting position—without skis on—and walk around the room for
about one minute. This ought to be repeated several times,

and afterward the position will not feel strange when going uphill on skis.)

We are now back on the snow on skis. The skier has not started up the hill yet. He is on the flats at the bottom of the slope.

The following leg motion for uphill climbing should be practiced while still on the flats.

This leg motion is not new. The technique is to extend the leg until the foot is slightly ahead of the knee when moving the ski forward. The ski is thus moved forward so that the toe is ahead of the knee. One of our students called it a "goose step."

While still on the flats, the skier should "sit down" about 3 inches lower than usual, and should then shuffle ahead by goose stepping. The forward ski will lift off the snow slightly. It is a motion similar to kicking a soccer ball.

Five or ten minutes should be spent doing this.

Now the skier should ski to the base of the slope—and shouldn't forget to sit down an extra 3 inches.

He should go up the hill only three or four steps—just to test out the-toe-ahead-of-the-knee technique. Notice what this does. When the forward-moving ski goes into the snow (with the toe pointing ahead), two important things naturally result: 1) at the end of the forward motion, the ski abruptly presses down on the snow; and 2) after the ski has been slapped or plopped down on the snow, the skier's weight automatically is transferred to the heel. (It can't do otherwise if the toe has been in front of the knee.) The ski—the entire length of it—is forced against the snow with considerable pressure. This locks the wax on the skis into the snow crystals, and the ski holds.

The skier should go up the slight slope at the base of the hill four or five steps. (He must make certain that the slope is gentle.) He should now turn around and come down. We insist on a gentle slope at this point so that the skier can get the feel of the climb, can turn easily, and come down. This should be done a dozen times until the skier not only feels comfortable with the movement, but also sees for himself that it works.

The skier now is ready to learn the full technique.

The full uphill technique consists of exactly what the skier already has done plus the use of the poles.

The poles are important in going uphill; they are used to help *push* the skier up the hill—to *push*, not pull.

The pole baskets should always be behind the skier. By doing this, the poles always will be lower and further back than when using them on the flats (*Figs. 3 and 4*).

Figs. 3 and 4

As the skier goes uphill, the poles are used mostly for one thing: to push. If one remembers this, everything else regarding pole motion will naturally be correct.

The skier should start up the hill with small steps.

He should not move a ski ahead unless both pole tips are in the snow. Their assistance is important in keeping balance.

One should not be able to see the hands, except on the periphery of the line of vision. If the hands are directly visible, they are too high and too far forward (*Fig.* 5).

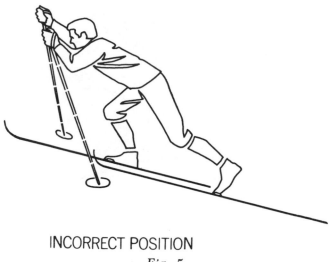

INCORRECT POSITION

Fig. 5

There must always be three points of contact on the ground: two poles and one ski (the one having most of the weight on it).

The skier should now go up the hill.

He should then turn around at the top and ski to the bottom.

This should be repeated several times.

Going up and down the gentle slope will soon bore the skier; and he will want to go to a steeper hill. But we suggest remaining on short hills until all the techniques of uphill climbing have been learned.

Uphill by Traversing

Traversing, basically, is the same technique as climbing straight up the hill.

Sometimes, however, the hill is too steep to go straight up. Instead, the skier, utilizing the same general uphill technique, zigzags, using the kick turn to turn from the end of a zig to the beginning of a zag (*Fig. 6*).

Fig. 6

How to traverse uphill: The skier should start at the bottom of a gentle slope, aiming the skis so that the angle at which he must climb will be a slight one. But, first, he must look up the hill and plan approximately how the zigzag path will go, utilizing the terrain to its best advantage.

The end of the first leg should be at a spot which seems to be one of the flatter areas of that part of the hill. The less steep the end of the first leg of the zigzag, the better. At this point, it will be necessary to make a turn to the next upward traverse. A kick turn can be used or the following simple step turn.

SIMPLE UPHILL STEP TURN

On gentle slopes, a simple uphill step turn may be effective for some skiers. In this maneuver, assuming that the end of a traverse has been reached and that it is now time to turn, the skier must first remember the low, bent-knee position mentioned earlier in the book; then, in a turn to the right, he must move the right pole down the hill and away from its normal placement attained earlier from the climbing position. With a majority of the weight on the left ski, the skier should slide the right ski ahead until the toe of that foot is ahead of the knee, and should swing the tip around until it is facing in the desired direction for the next uphill traverse (*Fig. 7*).

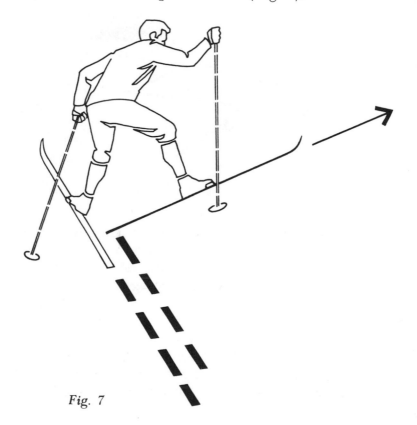

Fig. 7

The majority of the weight is now placed on the right ski, and the skier should make sure that the ski is slightly slapped in the snow and edged uphill to form a neat platform that will support *all* of the body weight.

Now with a majority of the weight on the right ski and right pole (it may be necessary to change the position of the right pole in order to feel comfortable) and still in a low and, therefore, safe position, the skier should slide the left ski slightly ahead to get the left toe in front of the left knee and should then swing the ski around and place it parallel to the right ski.

From here on in, it is easy to continue the traverse up the hill.

As always, if the skier can maintain a relatively low squat and avoid excessive bending at the waist, the turns can be executed with considerable ease.

Naturally, the turn to the left is done exactly the opposite.

Now, the skier must start up the hill at an angle, moving legs, skis, and poles exactly as if climbing straight up, with one exception: he must always have the uphill sides of the skis edged into the snow in order to stop from sliding downhill sideways (**Fig. 8**).

Hint: If the hill is so steep that the skier tends to slip backwards as he attempts the simple uphill step turn, then it is not the terrain on which to use it. In this case, use the kick turn (*see page 71*).

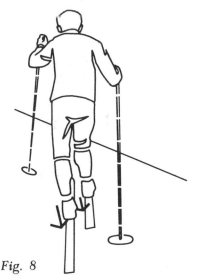

Fig. 8

The first leg of the zigzag (the zig) should be completed, and the skier should come to a stop.

A kick turn should be executed so that the skier is now facing in the opposite direction and the skis form a right angle with the fall line.

After doing this, the skier should look up the hill at an angle and choose the direction and length of the next leg of the traverse. He must remember not to traverse too steeply.

The skier now skis up the next leg.

Again, he stops.

Again, he kick-turns toward the opposite direction.

He continues up the hill by this same method, zigging up for one leg, stopping, turning, and then zagging up in the other direction.

It is very, very easy as long as the skier remembers to edge in the uphill side of the skis.

Uphill by Side Stepping

When using the side step, the skier and his tracks should resemble the skier and tracks shown in Figure 9. It can be practiced (for the first few practice climbs) on the same gentle slope that the skier has been using all along.

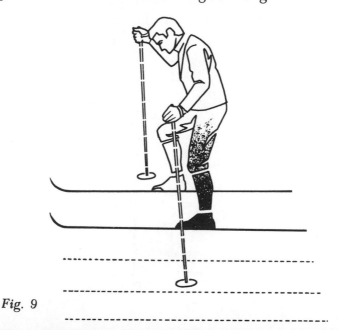

Fig. 9

(1) He should start at the bottom of the hill with the skis at right angle to the fall line. (The fall line is the path down which a snowball or boulder would roll if shoved off the top of the hill.) If the term "fall line" is confusing, then the skier should just remember to stand in a position which will always keep the skis horizontal to the slope as he side-

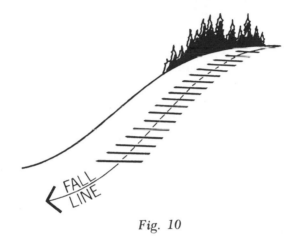

Fig. 10

steps up the hill (*Fig. 10*). No matter where the skier is on the hill as he is side stepping, his skis will always be on the horizontal, and there will be no inclination to slide downhill either forward or backward.

The skis should be about a foot apart, with the poles in their natural position—about a foot from the sides of the skis and about a foot in front of the boots. The skier should lean forward slightly so that a small portion of the body weight can rest on the poles.

The uphill pole is moved about 20 inches uphill, and the uphill ski is lifted about 8 inches off the ground—it should be raised up so that it is parallel to the ground, the tip and tail being the same distance from the snow.

The skier should move (step) the lifted ski uphill about 15 or 20 inches and slap it down onto the snow gently; and after slapping it down, should edge it into the snow to stop it from sliding downhill. The edge of the ski should bite firmly into the snow. To accomplish this, *the ankle is rolled slightly uphill*, into the hill.

The weight is now shifted to the uphill ski, and the downhill ski is moved uphill the same 15 or 20 inches. The lower ski is slapped and edged into the snow, while the skier rolls his ankle uphill to accomplish this so that the ski will not slip downhill. The skier should now shift his weight to the downhill ski and side-step up the hill with the uphill ski.

These movements should continue all the way up the hill; but once the climbing has started, it should be done rhythmically, moving the ski and the pole simultaneously.

(2) Occasionally, snow will pile up on the tips or tails of skis when side stepping. Should this occur, the skier should stop and shuffle the skis back and forth to free them and shake the snow off.

The side step for hill climbing is easy and safe. It is good for going up the steeper hills and steep, narrow trails. Even the steepest hills can be climbed with the side step. It is the natural way of going up a difficult slope.

The herringbone method of climbing (see p. 89) is also good for steep slopes and narrow trails, but it is the most tiring method of climbing.

When going up steep, narrow trails, we often vary from the side step to the herringbone for short distances, not only to increase the speed of ascent, but also to vary the body muscles which are being used and to create a change of pace. This helps to relax the body and diminish fatigue on a long tour.

THE TRAVERSE SIDE STEP

When the hill is both steep and wide, it is often advantageous to climb it using the traverse side step. This technique is precisely what its name indicates: a combination of side stepping and traversing. The skier does a side step up a hill, but the uphill ski is moved simultaneously *forward*. The downhill ski follows in the same direction. The skier should avoid taking large steps which overextend the body and lead to an unbalanced position (*Fig. 11*).

Fig. 11

The traverse side step is an easy and relaxing method of climbing steep, wide hills.

Uphill by Herringbone Climbing

This uphill technique is called the herringbone because that is what the tracks that are left behind in the snow look like. As with side stepping, the herringbone is a natural method of climbing steep slopes; and most skiers would learn it on their own if given the time and possessing the inclination to experiment.

To learn it quickly and properly, the skier should start off on a flat area.

(1) The tips of the skis are moved outward so that the tails form the closed section of a large "V." This time, the "V" is not the upside-down "V" of the snowplow (*Fig. 12*).

Fig. 12

(2) The skier should go forward, moving one ski ahead, and then the other. It is just like walking forward Charlie Chaplin style, with toes pointed outward.

(3) While walking forward in this manner, the inside edges of the skis should be rolled inward, the edges of the skis now biting into the snow.

Having the inside edges bite into the snow is not needed on the flats, but it is very important when climbing hills (*Fig. 13*).

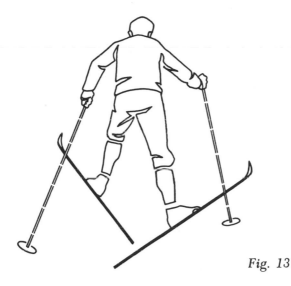

Fig. 13

It is more difficult to edge the skis on the flats than on the slopes; so if the skier does it a few times on the flat area, it will be easy when he gets on the slope.

(4) The skier now starts up the slope with the skis spread apart herringbone fashion and with the inside edges biting into the snow. The practice slope is gentle and the skier will have no trouble ascending it via herringbone. As the angle of the slope increases, it will be necessary to increase the angle of the herringbone—that is, the tips will have to be open more (*Fig. 14*). This will become obvious once the skier moves to the steeper hills.

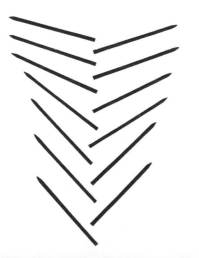

Fig. 14

(5) The skier must not bend forward when herringboning up a hill. If he has difficulty in avoiding bending forward, here is a way to break the inclination.

He should stand still after having taken a few herringbone steps up the hill—stand still and rest. The angle that the body naturally assumes when standing still is the same angle to assume when continuing up the hill.

(6) When herringboning up a hill, each ski should be planted into the snow with a slap. This will not only make the wax hold, but will also force the edge of the ski to bite into the snow.

(7) The baskets of both poles should be well behind (downhill of) the skis. The hands should be about waist high (*Fig. 15*).

Fig. 15

The poles are uphill pushers. For as long as the skier remembers that he is using the poles to help push himself uphill, the positioning of the poles will take care of itself naturally.

Hint: If the skis slip back while going uphill, the skier has either taken too large a step (note, in Figure 16, the out-

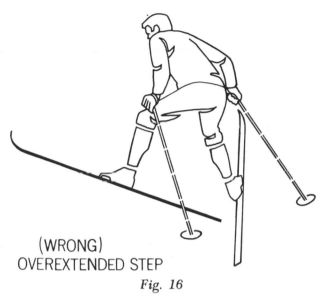

(WRONG)
OVEREXTENDED STEP
Fig. 16

stretched lower leg which leaves the skier in an unbalanced position), or the poles are not behind the skis and are not pushing forward, or the herringbone angle is not wide enough. Usually, a back slip is the result of too large a step, which reduces the angle of edge bite as well as that of ski spread.

Note: When moving uphill with deep tracks in deep snow, the "half-herringbone" is used. This is a herringbone with a lesser angle and a slightly longer step.

11

Conclusion of Novice Section

When the skier has gotten this far in his lessons, he will have learned

(1) how to move with confidence across flat terrain;

(2) how to make a step turn on the flats and change direction;

(3) how to ski down hills;

(4) how to turn while skiing down hills by using the a) step turn, and b) half-snowplow turn;

(5) how to make a kick turn on both the flats and the hills; and

(6) how to go uphill by a) straight climbing, b) traverse

climbing, c) side-step traversing, d) side stepping, and e) her-ringboning.

The beginner is *no longer a beginner*. He is now an intermediate and is ready to learn some of the more sophisticated tech-

Fig. 1

niques of cross-country skiing. And, much to his joy, he will find that what follows will be easier and even more fun to learn than the things he has already mastered (way back when he was a rank novice, a beginner).

PART **II**

INTERMEDIATE TECHNIQUE

12

The Kick

In previous lessons, the skier was taught how to move forward on skis by shuffling ahead.

Shuffling forward is good for novices, but once the skier has his ski legs, he should learn how to "kick" himself ahead. It is this technique which makes it possible to cover long distances with ease and speed. With each kick, the skier glides forward. The longer and faster each glide, the more distance is covered with the least amount of effort.

It is easiest to learn the kick by practicing it in a well-set track.

How to Make a Track

With skis about 8 inches apart, the skier should shuffle forward for about 50 yards.

He now looks back.

In the snow will be two tracks, 8 inches apart, which were made by the skis.

The skier should now shuffle back and forth over those tracks about six times until the track is well set.

The kick should be practiced in a well-set track because the track will prevent any side slipping and will let the skier concentrate on moving himself ahead. The track "steers" the ski.

Learning the Kick

The skier should stand at one end of the track and hold the poles any way which is comfortable. There is a specific way to use them, but this will be discussed later.

The left ski is moved about a foot ahead of the right one. The knees should be slightly bent.

The weight is put on the right ski.

Now, the skier should hop ahead (yes! we said "hop") from

Fig. 1

the right ski to the left ski (*Fig. 1*). In hopping to the left ski, two things happen: 1) the weight is shifted to the left ski; and 2) the left ski slides forward in the track. The skier moves ahead, not only the distance of the hop, but also of the glide.

When the left ski begins to stop gliding, the skier should then hop from the left ski to the right ski.

By going down the track in this manner—hopping forward from one ski to the other, and sliding forward with each hop—the skier must consciously get the feeling of shifting weight

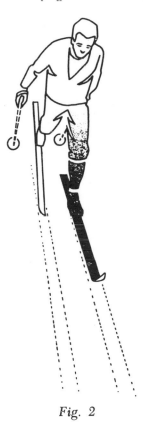

Fig. 2

from one ski to the other as he hops (*Fig. 2*). And after each hop, there must be a forward slide. For the time being, he should not worry about the kicking ski but should simply "hop" off it. Concentration should be directed toward shifting the weight to the forward, or sliding, ski and balancing all one's weight on it. The object is to get a long slide out of the maneuver—to get "for nothing" as much forward motion as is possible. One should not worry about the position of the "kick-off" ski: it will come back to the snow on its own. Racers carry the kick-off ski high and off the snow. But this will come with experience.

The skier should go back and forth in the track about a dozen times, hopping smoothly from one ski to the other and sliding after each hop.

Now, leaving poles behind, the skier should stand at the end of the track, with the left ski about a foot ahead of the right.

Most of the body weight should be put on the left ski. The skier should pretend that the left ski is a scooter. With that ski being the scooter, the other foot (ski) is used to push it along the track (*Figs. 3 and 4*).

Figs. 3 and 4

Push and slide, push and slide—always keeping the left ski in front and using the right one as the pusher.

By doing this, two things will be made obvious: 1) that the skier can push or "kick" himself forward; and 2) that balance is involved, and that it is easy to maintain it as long as the body weight is shifted to the sliding ski.

The left ski, in this manner, is pushed the length of the track.

The process should now be reversed by putting the right ski in front and pushing with the left foot. Some beginners find it helpful to place both hands on the knees of the forward leg when pushing with the other: this tends to place the body in the correct position.

This should be done several times, switching the "pusher ski" at each end of the track.

Now, still without poles, the skier should go back and forth over the track, alternating—pushing first with one ski and then with the other. The skier (without poles) is now really hopping from one ski to the other. With practice and with poles, he will later be able—instead of pushing—to thrust, hop, or kick himself ahead with ease and speed. Now, take the poles.

Using poles to assist in balancing, the skier should practice hopping back and forth along the track—left foot, to right foot, to left foot, and so on—holding each glide as long as possible, but starting the next hop just before the glide stops.

To do the kick well and efficiently, it is necessary to use the poles properly; and this correct method is diagonal poling, and is given in the next lesson.

13

The Diagonal Stride

The stride most frequently used is called "the diagonal" because the right leg and left pole (and vice versa) work together.

When the skier kicks himself ahead from his right foot, he also pushes himself ahead with his left pole (*Fig. 1*). This technique makes for greater forward thrust and easy balance.

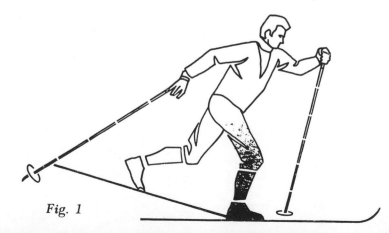

Fig. 1

It sounds difficult, but it actually is the most natural way to swing the arms and legs, even when walking.

Here is proof.

The skier should walk or shuffle ahead on the skis, swinging the arms and dragging the poles. The right arm and the left leg will swing forward at the same time naturally, just as the right leg and the left arm will do.

Walking or shuffling the length of the track, the skier should swing his arms, holding the poles loosely by the straps in order to become conscious of how the left arm and right leg move together, and of how right arm and left leg move together.

The skier should then go the length of the track, hopping forward instead of shuffling. When he hops off his left leg, he then also pushes back with his right pole (*Fig. 2*).

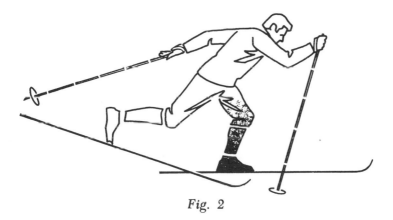

Fig. 2

That's all there is to the basic diagonal stride.

The skier must practice, practice, practice this to make sure that the opposite legs and poles are pushing simultaneously. This should be practiced only on the flats at first, where the forward speed will be fairly constant. With constant speed, the skier will pick the right place in the snow to thrust the pole and begin his forward push with it.

The diagonal stride is also used for uphill climbing. In this case, the pole thrusts will be shorter because the skier's steps are shorter.

Hint: When diagonalling, one ought not to permit the pole to swing or pendulum forward during the glide. It must be carried forward willfully by the skier.

14

Double Poling

The technique of double poling is simple. Both arms are placed straight out in front of the skier. With the poles hanging down almost vertically, the points are thrust into the snow

Fig. 1

(*Fig. 1*) and the skier pushes back with both poles simultaneously (*Fig. 2*)—as far back as possible—and then brings them
forward and repeats the operation.

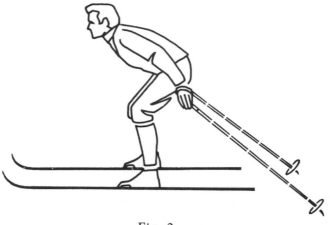

Fig. 2

Double poling is useful when coming down gentle slopes if
the skier wishes to increase his speed. It is also useful on
the flats as a means of breaking monotony after using diagonal
poling for some time, and for pushing over rolls and bumps.

Double poling is fun. Its effectiveness depends largely on
the build of the skier—on arm and shoulder strength. Everyone
should double pole at least a little; it varies the muscles used,
thus providing relaxation and rest.

PART **III**

ADVANCED TECHNIQUE

15

The Perfected Kick

The quickest way of identifying an expert skier is by observing his diagonal technique, particularly his kick and the long glide which follows.

Expert cross-country skiers, especially racers, develop techniques for the purpose of covering maximum distances with the least expenditure of time and energy. The characteristics of this accomplishment are the long strides, the glide, the smoothness, the relaxation, and the effective kick.

By this time, the reader already knows enough about the kick and the glide to cover long distances with comfort and ease. Now we will demonstrate how to cover distances with speed and still greater ease.

We are not trying to persuade the reader to become a cross-country racer and a candidate for the U. S. Olympic Team. But, we want to make available the techniques used by these experts.

The Expert's Kick

To learn the expert's kick, it is first necessary to prepare a practice track. The track consists of a double path made by skis in the snow. It should be about a quarter to a half a mile long, and shaped either like a circle or a loop. Most of it should be on flat ground; but it is advantageous if there is some rolling terrain for some of the track. This is helpful because the skier can practice the kick going up an incline. Also, he can practice resting while going down an incline, as well as resting by changing pace on the flat. Some readers may not have the space available to make the perfect track. In that event, the minimum usable track is a straight path about 60 yards long.

The way to make the track is to ski around the circle or the loop or the short, straight line. The skis should make two paths in the snow, approximately 8 inches apart and from 1 inch to 2 inches deep. The track is made by repeatedly skiing over the same two paths. If the snow is powdery, make the track one day and allow it to stand overnight before beginning a serious practice of the kick. It is necessary for the track to have a solid base from which to kick.

There are three reasons for having a track:

(1) It provides a snow base of consistent texture from which it is possible to obtain maximum kick. Also, since the snow texture in the track will be consistent, it is possible to maintain maximum wax-effectiveness.

(2) A track makes it possible for the ski to glide along after the weight shift has been made. It also assists in the steering of the ski, thus making it easier for the skier to get a long glide after the weight shift has been made.

(3) The track helps the skier maintain his balance and prevents lateral movement of the skis.

Earlier in the book the skier learned that after the kick (and as a result of it), all of his weight had to be transferred to the gliding ski—the forward ski. We wish to remind the skier of this, because the basic element of the successful kick is the complete weight shift to the ski on which the glide will take place (the forward ski; *Fig. 1*).

Fig. 1

Until the expert's kick becomes second nature, it will require concentration to learn the complete weight shift well. The explosiveness of the expert's kick requires a higher degree of balance than the ordinary touring kick.

Let's begin.

The poles should be left behind. With the skis on, the skier should stand in the track and shuffle ahead in the manner described on pages 43–44. At this point, the skis should not be lifted from the snow. At all times, the skis must be firmly on the track.

The skier should shuffle ahead slowly and with extra-long steps; this will require a deeper bending of the knees than is done in ordinary touring. When this feels comfortable (which should be after five or six steps), he should then accentuate moving the body from side to side while shuffling ahead.

The upper part of the body should be moved so that the head is directly over the *forward* ski and about a foot ahead of the toe of the boot. As each ski alternates with the other and becomes the forward ski, the position of the body and head should also shift from one side to the other.

As the skier shuffles forward, he will be moving his head and the upper part of his body from side to side, but with the head always ending up over the forward ski (*Fig. 2*).

Fig. 2

At first, this feels absurd indeed; but this exercise should be continued for a minimum of five minutes. When the rhythm of upper part of the body becomes regular, then the skier's concentration should be shifted to pronounced flexing of knees— so much so that after five minutes, the muscles in the thigh (or upper leg) will feel strained (*Fig. 3*).

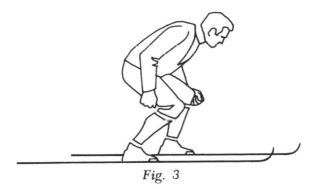

Fig. 3

After doing a simple shuffle as described, the skier must now do what is called the "speed shuffle." The only difference between the speed shuffle and the one that has already been done is that we want the skier to glide, glide, glide ahead on the forward ski while thinking, "I'm going to get a longer glide; I'm going to get a longer glide." This requires a harder push-off from the aft or thrusting ski.

We will, from now on, turn some of our teaching terminology into racing terminology. The ski which we have spoken of as the "forward ski" will from now on be referred to as the "gliding ski." The ski that we have spoken of as the "nonforward ski" or the "back ski" or the "pushing ski" will be always known as the "kicking ski."

The skier is now speed shuffling, shifting all his weight to the gliding ski. He is producing long, long glides.

After this has been done for a few minutes, the skier now can lift the kicking ski off the snow at the end of each kick. Once the skier kicks backward with force, the natural inclination is to lift the tail of the kicking ski at the completion of each kick.

As the kick becomes perfected, there is *no conscious lifting of the ski whatever!* The force of a powerful kick is directed practically straight down on the track. After the kick, the leg goes into the follow-through phase, continues on back until nearly straight, and is completely relaxed. *The tip of the kicking ski* never leaves the snow, but the tail will be from 1 foot to 2 feet off the ground (*Fig. 4*).

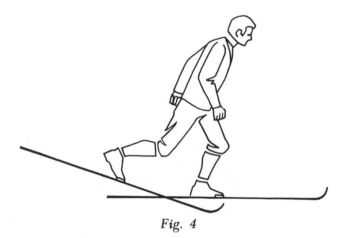

Fig. 4

The skier has begun the expert's kick (remembering that during this practice exercise the poles are not being used). This is an important exercise and we recommend that he practice it for about a half hour.

It would be very helpful, indeed, if a companion went along who could compare the skier's movements with those of the illustrations.

The skier will go from one ski to the other *before he has completely stopped gliding*. This comes so naturally that there is no need for us to elaborate on it.

There will be no doubt in the skier's mind about when to

change the order of the skis, since it is a natural motion. But as a matter of definition, it should be remembered that the skier should always have forward motion. The kick and the weight shift must be done before the glide stops. The forward momentum should never be lost.

The skier may lose his balance occasionally while all his weight is on the gliding ski. Balance can be regained by shifting weight to the other ski and using the gliding ski to push off. This amounts to nothing more than doing the next kick earlier than usual.

The major purpose of these fifteen minutes of practice is to provide the skier with the knowledge of how to move ahead on the gliding ski with all his weight on it. At the end of about fifteen minutes, the intermediate skier should feel comfortable, gliding ahead with his total weight on the gliding ski. At this point, each glide should be several feet long; and the skier should experience the satisfaction of "getting something for nothing."

The arms: At this stage of practice, the skier should not even think about the arms, but should let them hang down loose, swinging easily and naturally.

If, after a half an hour, the skier does not feel comfortable in his glide and balance, he should stop and rest a few hours. If he feels awkward or slow, it may be because the snow in the track isn't properly packed, or because the wax needs correcting, or because the skier is cold or tired. But, with everything going well, he should have it in about half an hour. By "having it," we mean that the skier should have been able to acquire good balance and a comfortable glide in the speed shuffle. Often, skiers must repeat the exercise many times. Experts practice continually.

If, at the end of the half hour, the skier is comfortable and secure, he will notice that: 1) the shoulder which is over the weighted or gliding ski is dropped a few inches with each kick; and 2) the hip which is over the gliding ski has been moved slightly down and forward with each kick (*Fig. 5*). A

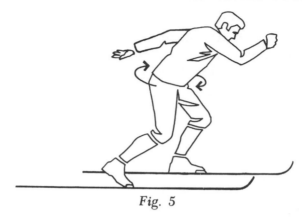

Fig. 5

good cross-country racer will end up at the end of each kick with his hips at approximately a 45° angle to the track. The skier learning the kick should not force the hip angulation. It will come a little at the beginning, naturally—enough to be noticeable. As a strong kick and a long glide are developed, the hip angulation will increase on its own.

The Actual Kick

What has been described is the preparation for learning the actual kick.

If the skier is fatigued or uncomfortable after his speed-shuffling exercise, we suggest that he wait for the next day before starting the next lesson. An advanced skier or someone who is in excellent physical condition should have no problems and will be able to continue.

The skier is still practicing without the use of his poles.

He should begin by doing five or six steps of the speed shuffle, just to get comfortable, and should then get ready to make the first real expert's kick.

Almost at the end of a glide, there is a natural inclination to hop over onto the other ski. The skier now gets himself into a position on the forward foot called "rolling up." Actually, there is no rolling up at all since the boot must stay flat on the ski. But the sensation is one of "rolling up." It involves bending the forward knee slightly more than is usual, and moving the body ahead over it more than feels natural. The skier is "coiling up" to spring onto the other ski (*Fig. 6*).

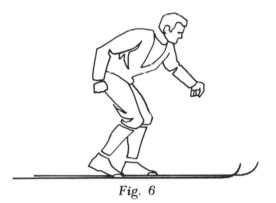

Fig. 6

When the skier has "rolled up," with a mighty hop, he then kicks himself ahead and onto the other ski. This involves 1) kicking the ski which had been the gliding ski back as explosively as he can manage it; 2) moving his head, shoulders, and weight over to the other ski; and 3) gliding as long as is comfortable on the new gliding ski.

If the skier is doing this properly, he will have the sensation that the actual kick starts as the foot which is moving forward passes the gliding ski. This, however, is not quite how it happens. The kick begins a little earlier than this. The skier must consciously begin his kick when the forward foot is 3 or 4 inches in front of the other one.

The first few times that the skier tries this powerful kick, he may find it awkward. This is only because he is unable at the beginning to judge the amount of power which he is able to put into the kick while still maintaining his balance. Normally, after three or four minutes of practice he is able to know how much power can be exerted.

The first thing he will notice is that at the end of the kick, the rear leg (which, from now on, will be called the "carried ski") is fully extended (*Fig. 7*). (*The remainder of the illustrations will show how the movements look with the skier using his poles—even though the exercise should be practiced without the poles.*)

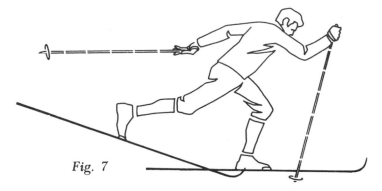

Fig. 7

As the skier is gliding ahead on the gliding ski, the tail of the carried ski will be about 20 inches off the snow and its tip will be sliding along in its track.

The back-kick motion is called by the experts a "bang." This is a good descriptive expression for what happens.

Besides the backward part of the bang, the skier will remember that the hips end up at a 45° angle to the track. This is accomplished by a vigorous, twisting thrust of the pelvis. Not only does this help in maintaining balance, but it also adds to the forward momentum.

At the end of the kick, or bang, the skier's back is in a slightly arched position (*Fig. 8*). He will have the feeling that he is coiling and uncoiling.

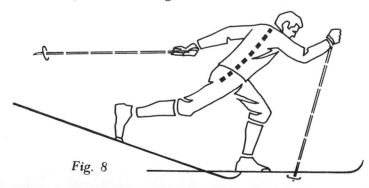

Fig. 8

If the glide, the kick, and the weight shift are done properly, the carried ski will remain the "carried ski" and will not be flat on the snow again until it passes the other foot as it is getting ready to do its own kick (*Fig.* 9). It will be carried throughout the glide and during the time when the body is coiling up in preparation for the next kick.

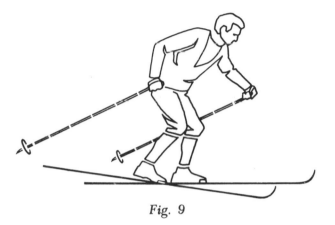

Fig. 9

If the carried ski starts to come down too early or is not carried naturally, it is an indication that there has not been a clean kick and complete weight shift.

Also, if the ski is not carried as we just described and comes forward and slaps down on the snow early before it passes the other foot, it then acts as a drag, slowing down the skier and breaking his rhythm.

A good exercise to practice is to stand in the track (without poles) and to swing the arms back and forth in pole-swinging motion, co-ordinating each swing with a bending of the knees. It is a *half* deep-knee bend. The head is swung slightly from side to side, but the eyes are always looking ahead down the track.

If the skier, in practicing the kick (without poles), experiences any difficulty, he should then practice it exactly as he did the scooter exercise as described earlier (*Fig. 10*).

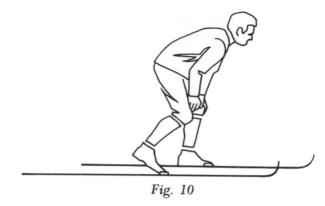

Fig. 10

The skier must practice for about a week without poles (for an hour a day, at least). He will then be ready to use the poles.

He should not get discouraged if the poleless technique does not come easily. Even Olympic competitors practice this technique for a couple of hours daily.

16

Advanced Diagonalling and Uphill Running

After the skier has learned the perfected kick without poles, he then has to learn it with poles. Although there are several techniques on how to use the poles when running along with the kick, the one that is used most often is called "diagonalling." This is what we are going to learn now. Diagonalling has been renamed single sticking by some racers (*Fig. 1*). In any case, it is the total action of the legs, arms, and poles.

Fig. 1

If the skier finds it awkward to use the poles by diagonalling, it means that he has not practiced his kick and weight shift sufficiently, and should go back and practice it without the poles.

The skier already knows simple diagonalling for normal ski touring; the principle is the same for fast skiing, merely refined for efficiency.

The pole is planted in the snow in preparation for using it to push the skier ahead in conjunction with the kick of the opposite foot.

The arm is bent, forming a 90° angle. The first motion after the pole has been planted ahead is a slight drop of the shoulder. This shoulder drop is the beginning of the arm thrust. Its function is to add strength and rhythm to the pole thrust. The shoulder drop is part of the "coiling up."

From this position, the skier pushes himself forward from the planted pole. This is done simultaneously with the back kick of the opposite leg (*Fig. 2*).

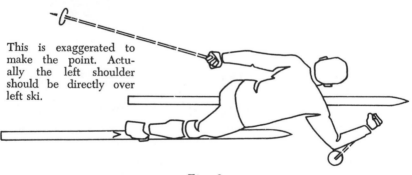

This is exaggerated to make the point. Actually the left shoulder should be directly over left ski.

Fig. 2

At the end of the pole thrust, the arm is pointing backward. The hand is relaxed, resting for the next push. With the last three fingers of the hand opened on the shaft, the pole is held loosely only by the thumb and the forefinger with the strap wrapped around the wrist (*Fig. 3*).

Fig. 3

The pushing phase of that pole maneuver is now ended; and the skier (who is gliding ahead on the opposite ski) is getting ready to bring the pole forward.

The bringing forward of the pole is initiated by a slight drop

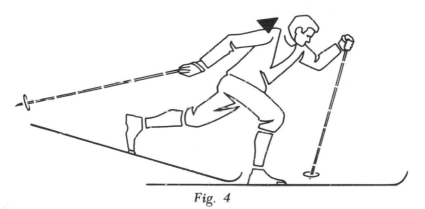

Fig. 4

of the shoulder (*Fig. 4*). The arm is brought forward—straight and totally relaxed—in a pendulum motion until it reaches the midpoint, pointing toward the ground. It continues to swing forward and up. As it comes forward and up, it begins to bend until it is at a 90° angle, and is ready to be planted into the snow once more. During this forward-swinging motion, the arm is extended fully and is relaxed.

The skier quickly realizes here that both shoulders, while striding or diagonalling, drop simultaneously. One is forward, one is back, but both drop. This drop is part of the "uncoiling" process.

Uphill Running

Basically, advanced diagonal uphill technique is similar to advanced diagonalling on the flats. But in diagonalling uphill speedily, the body sinks lower. Also the steps are faster and shorter. This is necessary because the steep uphill grade causes the "free" glide to diminish. Naturally the "free" glide is less going uphill than on a flat terrain.

The racer should not wear himself out with an initial burst of speed (causing slowing and puffing at the end of the spurt). The skier should choose a tempo which can be maintained constantly all the way up; this tempo should leave the racer enough energy to continue at a fast rate after reaching the top.

17

Advanced Double Poling

Skiing with the diagonal-poling method is the technique most used in cross-country. Over long distances it is easiest and fastest for sustained effort, though it can become monotonous. Furthermore, a frequent pace-change or stride-change is advantageous—and more than being advantageous, it is necessary, because one should not overtire any one set of muscles.

One of the best methods of "changing stride" is by temporarily changing from diagonal poling to double poling. Although double poling is more strenuous, it can provide bursts of speed and allows the muscles used in diagonal poling to rest, especially those of the arms, shoulders, and back.

Terrain Where the Double Pole is Used

Double poling can be used on practically any terrain except uphill. It is used most frequently on slight downgrades or on a "humpy" section of track; occasionally in conjunction with gliding steps. Many strong racers, however, frequently use it on the flats. Racers and tourers often find double poling convenient.

The choice of places and times to use double poling is a personal one decided on by the skier after much practice. Skiers with extra-powerful arms and shoulders, for example, are inclined to double pole more than skiers with normal physiques.

The timing and method of entering into the double pole is determined by the pitch of the slope (the terrain), depth of the snow, and the effectiveness of the wax. Also, the skier must decide whether he will double pole while running (using the kick) or with both skis flat on the snow. This is done intuitively rather than by conscious decisions.

The skier may feel that the diagonal is awkward and will realize that much forward gliding "for nothing" is available to him by double poling and without kicking.

The Steps of the Double Pole

There are several methods used in double poling. One of the easiest, naturally, will be when the skier is gliding down a slope—without kicking—and wishes some additional assistance.

In this double-pole maneuver, both arms are swung forward simultaneously and the baskets are allowed to pendulum for-

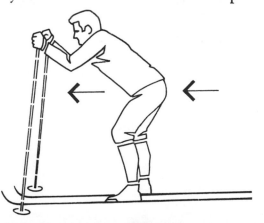

Fig. 1

ward a bit (*Fig. 1*). (The only time in cross-country skiing that
the poles are allowed to swing forward is during the double-
pole maneuver). After the poles are placed in the forward position, they are planted in the snow, and much upper-body

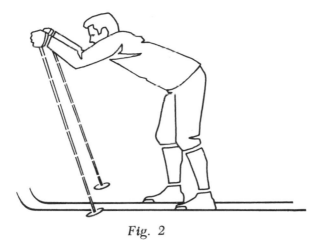

Fig. 2

weight is put on them (*Fig. 2*). The skier then pushes the poles
vigorously to the rear, using both arms.

  The more energy put into the push, the greater the resulting
speed. The hands pass close to and slightly below the knees.
The chest will go down and almost touch the thighs (*Fig. 3*).

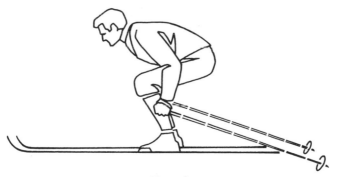

Fig. 3

This is a good time to exhale vigorously; and as the body rises on the follow-through, the skier should inhale just as vigorously.

The follow-through consists of allowing the arms to swing to the rear, and the shoulders, arms, and hands to relax (*Fig. 4*).

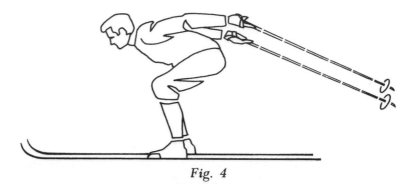

Fig. 4

At this point, the upper half of the body starts to rise, and many good racers even straighten up fully, throwing their shoulders back and arching their backs slightly, thereby allowing mental and physical relaxation (*Fig. 5*).

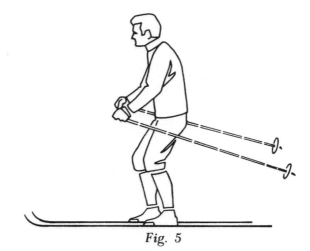

Fig. 5

Double Poling with Double Steps

Double poling is probably most often entered into by using at least two or three gliding steps during which the poles are carried. The skier straightens his back slightly, and as the two or three quick steps are taken, both arms are brought forward, the baskets are allowed to pendulum, and then the pole plant is made (*Fig. 6*). Depending upon the amount of forward

Fig. 6

speed, the poles may go into the snow quite a bit beyond the vertical (see the illustration). The push and follow-through are the same as previously described.

Some racers who have particularly strong torsos and upper shoulders use this double-pole step frequently on the flats. Even though it requires more strength to execute, it is an effective way of changing stride, of resting one set of muscles, and of gaining speed.

All skiers should use some form of double poling as a change of pace. Unfortunately for them, many racers fail to use it enough when racing.

Double Poling with the Single Step

This is a subtle variation of the step just described. It is fun and extremely helpful on some types of terrain—generally where there are occasional bumps in the track, or where there are slight downgrades. Obviously only one quick, powerful step is taken before the poles pendulum out and are planted.

The single steps can also be taken from either leg. Some skiers have a favorite kicking leg which is used most of the

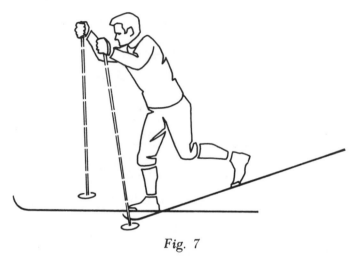

Fig. 7

time (*Fig. 7*). Others alternate legs naturally, double poling in between. For example, a skier could be moving along, kicking first with the right leg, double poling, gliding, then kicking with the left leg and double poling. When done in succession and well, it is like a beautifully executed dance. The terrain usually dictates which step is best. This technique of varying stride can be used until either mood or terrain change.

Hints: (1) We wish to emphasize the sequence of pole plant, push, and follow-through mentioned earlier. A great feeling of invigoration, looseness, and speed will result from the proper use of all these double-pole steps. It is a great time to stretch and relax. Racers should memorize these paces.

(2) If it is a "fast" day, a great deal of double poling may be done; but if it is a "slow" day, very little may be done.

(3) The skier should always ride out any forward momentum until it seems natural to execute some type of additional movement that will sustain motion.

(4) Good body position as well as good co-ordination with the stride and the double-pole push are extremely important. If the body stays high prior to the simultaneously executed kick and push, if the kick and push are well timed, and if the kicking ski is *kicked through* as the body weight goes onto the poles, an effective maneuver will be the result.

Double Poling Across Bumps and Dips

Running Bumps in series: On almost any track, slight rolls and bumps will develop. There is a smooth, fast, efficient way to progress over these. Experience and personal ability will generally dictate which techniques to use.

We have already mentioned that double poling (with or without steps) is the technique usually used on such terrain. We now wish to emphasize a small technical point (regardless of the step used, this next fact is important in skiing over bumps and dips on the flats).

We wish to remind the skier that he should always be looking down the track, constantly assessing the conditions that are coming up.

As the skier slides down into a dip, all his weight must be transferred to one ski (the dominant ski—everybody has one; Fig. 8). When that weighted ski is almost exactly at the bottom of the dip, the skier springs forcefully to the other ski. In anticipation of this spring, both poles have been allowed to pendulum forward. They are planted near the top of the next bump; the double-pole maneuver begins; and the skier passes up and over the bump.

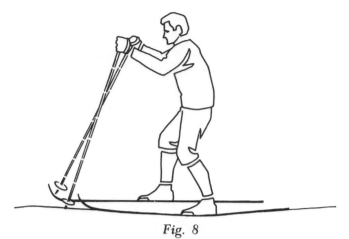

Fig. 8

It should be remembered that the strong flexibility in the tail of the ski is there to propel the skier quickly ahead as he goes down into a dip; but that at a point, if the weight is left on that ski, the skier will be trying to glide uphill (on the front side of the next bump) and will thus lose efficiency.

The tip of the ski is flexible, and will easily absorb the initial bending in the dip; but at a certain point, it, too, will start acting as a brake.

When the step to the unweighted ski is taken, the skier has done everything possible to reduce inefficiency to a minimum. The bump or dip should be crossed in one double pole. If this isn't possible, apply the following technique.

Running Bumps and Dips in Series

We have described how to cross bumps and dips by double poling out. This applies to a large bump or dip which can be done in one double pole. In a series of bumps and dips, the beginner will naturally try to double pole over all, and will fall into a series of unplanned (and slowing) passgangs. For a series of bumps and dips, the expert will maintain an easy, fast diagonal—and the uneven terrain will help him increase speed.

18

The Skate Turn

The skate turn not only changes direction but also increases speed. It can be used both on flats and on moderate downhill. Pick up the ski (the one in the direction you wish to turn in) and thrust about in the desired direction, meanwhile pushing off with the other ski. The push-off is a stretch motion; and it should be a straight line from skier's head to outside ankle. Then pick up the behind ski and swing it around parallel to the first ski. This is usually followed by a double-pole stroke.

19

The Change-Up or Passgang

For going up inclines on a good track, there is another technique which is extremely simple to execute but difficult to describe. It is referred to as the "change-up" or passgang. The term "change-up" should not be confused with a change of stride, which has been mentioned earlier. They are very different.

This maneuver or technique is generally used moving up a long, relatively hard climb when an individual is attempting to "move out" or make time (in other words, it is primarily for racers). The skier will naturally be doing the diagonal up this incline.

The upper body is raised, the back is straight, and the poles are carried through three quick gliding steps without being used.

One pole (either one will do) is then casually dropped by the side in a sort of half-poling motion, while the other pole swings forward to resume the normal diagonal-poling action. During the three quick steps, the skier should arch his back if necessary or comfortable, should exhale and breathe deeply, and should then resume diagonalling.

In order for this technique to work well, the skier's wax must be working well. During the execution of the three quick steps the skier must retain a good, low, bent-knee position. This technique can be used many times on the same uphill, but after each time, the skier must go back to the diagonal for a few strides before the step can be repeated again. The same advantages result from this step as they did when the skier straightened up from the diagonal on the flat and used the double pole (i.e., the relaxing of hands, arms, and shoulders, as well as easier breathing).

This technique usually requires the on-the-spot assistance of an able coach before it can be mastered.

Some racers find this an extremely helpful step and use it frequently. Others seldom use it. When mastered, it provides a great feeling of casualness, finesse, and power.

Notes: The passgang is usually effective for up-climbing, but a similar technique is used a great deal by Norwegian racers on long, flat lakes. It is called the "almost-passgang," and consists of half-diagonal strides.

Both the passgang and almost-passgang have three advantage: they help (1) increase tempo; (2) allow variation of muscles used, by resting some while using others; (3) provide a way of adapting to terrain while holding constant speed..

20

Faster Downhill on Cross-Country Skis

By now, the skier, probably on his own, has gone down some rather steep hills, and at a fairly high rate of speed. In passing from the stage where the skier is on low hills to where he is on steep hills, he will discover that the change is mostly a psychological one. As he improves his balance and his certitude, he naturally becomes more and more daring. But we feel it highly appropriate to remind the skier that he can gain considerable advantage from practicing some of the almost obvious exercises and techniques used by the racers. For example: before starting downhill, he should breathe deeply a few times, bend the knees, shake the fingers as if each were a piece of string, and make sure that every part of his body, except those few muscles needed for standing, is absolutely relaxed. A real pro will be in such perfect balance that every muscle is automatically relaxed anyway.

The skier already knows about slowing and turning so that they will be executed almost automatically. He should imagine that his knees are shock absorbers. The upper part of the body travels with very little up-and-down motion, while the "shock absorber" knees go up and down as the skier goes over bumps

Fig. 1

and hollows. *The skier must always stay balanced and be ready to anticipate (Fig. 1) changes in terrain or snow.*

The skier has undoubtedly acquired the habit of having one ski always ahead of the other, the heel of the one boot being opposite the toe of the other. When the terrain becomes very rough or the skier sees that he is going into loose snow, he should then make sure that the forward ski is as much as 18 inches ahead.

High-Speed Turns

High-speed parallel turns are possible with cross-country skis, but even experts avoid attempting them unless conditions are nearly ideal—i.e., a packed surface with some loose snow, a wide slope, and reasonably smooth terrain.

Sometimes under such conditions it takes a keen eye to distinguish a good cross-country skier from an alpine skier. There is, however, a difference. The cross-country skier will probably be crouched slightly lower, may occasionally initiate his turns with a slight stem, and will always have his weight slightly back. In skiing downhill, the cross-country skier must always maintain a solid "feel" of his skis through the heel of the foot. This is the point where the critical aspect of turning the cross-country ski—the "edging"—is controlled.

To perfect the edging for high-speed turns, begin by practicing on easy slopes with snow which is not packed. Experiment by rolling the ankles first into the slope and then away from the slope. These alternate movements will demonstrate how easily the ski can "bite" into the snow.

When skiing traversely downhill, it is easy to observe whether the skis have been edged sufficiently. Simply look back at the ski-track made in the snow. If the skis have been edged enough, the track in the snow will be straight and sharp—two straight, parallel lines traversing down the slope. But if the angle of "bite" has not been enough, the sideslip of the skis will be obvious. Instead of straight, clean tracks, there will be a blurred, broad "sweep-up" of a path—which shows that the skis were slipping, sliding downhill—instead of a clean, two-line track.

The high-speed parallel turns are accomplished by changing the edging and shifting the weight. For example, if traversing downhill to the left, the left edges of both skis bite into the hill, and the weight is more on the right ski than on the left. By alternating the edging so that the right side of the ski bites into the snow, and by shifting the weight to the left ski, the skis will quickly turn from a left traverse to a straight down-hill and then to a right traverse, thus producing a parallel turn. There is forward motion during this maneuver, therefore the shifting of the edging is gradual—one edge of skis biting, to both skis flat, to the other edge biting.

Many other aspects of turning are similar to those in alpine downhill skiing: weight on the downhill ski, weight shift, edg-ing, angulation, opening up to the hill, etc. If the skier's bal-ance is good, his feet may be placed as close together as those of an alpine skier.

21

Relaxing on Long Tours

The mark of a good cross-country skier is his rhythmic, relaxed style. As he moves ahead, he seems to be getting an enormous forward glide "for nothing." Every muscle in his body appears to be relaxed except for those being used to push him ahead.

The skier must remember, however, that it is not necessary to hurry or race. Each individual will have his own pace and goal, and each tour will have a different objective. He should do that which is most enjoyable and which suits his individual needs.

By now, many aspects of skiing should have become second nature to the skier.

If he is going on a long tour, plans should be made well in advance. The skier ought to think about the equipment that might be necessary for a long haul or for an emergency. He should be sure to take along some extra clothing, a map, a compass, some quick-energy foods and drinks, and, above all, an aluminum ski tip for emergencies to replace a broken tip.

If the skier decides to go on a several-days ski-touring camping trip, there are books available which give suggestions for logical planning. He ought to arrange it so that all the skiers on the tour are of about equal ability. If it is a family tour, the skiing speed should accommodate that of the slowest member.

If someone should fall behind, under no circumstance should he be left alone. Naturally, the individual is already tired, and tiredness and confusion will be rapidly compounded in such a situation.

From a physical standpoint, the skier should not become overwhelmed by circumstances or the elements. He should remember that there is always *some* kind of solution to any problem! The skier should remain loose and adaptable.

The head should be kept up; the skier should not look down to watch his skis. Looking down is fatiguing, and soon all effort becomes heavy labor.

The eyes should be relaxed. Moving the eyes sideways and up and down keeps them relaxed. One method of relaxing the eyes is to enjoy the landscape, observing the beauty of the snow, the trees, and the clouds. Naturally, this will make for much greater skiing pleasure. When one ski tours, one does not fight nature. Quite the contrary, one enhances and works in harmony with it.

Resting or Conserving Energy on Various Types of Terrain

Flats: Just as a reminder, the skier should remember to use the double pole which has been described, and should constantly take advantage of the terrain. By this we mean keeping the head up, analyzing the terrain, and taking advantage of a free glide wherever possible.

Downhills: One of the first things to remember regarding resting on downhills, is to rest the mind. The skier ought not become overwhelmed by steep downhills. If it is too steep and terrifying, he should simply *side-step* down a ways! If it is open enough, he should start down on a diagonal. Advantage should be taken of terrain such as plateaus, upgrades, etc.

The skier should look for deep snow on the sides of the trail. If he is going too fast straight downhill, there are several ways of slowing:

(1) Snowplowing (see page 51). But this is not advantageous when in deep snow or when going downhill at high speed.

(2) If one is on an open hill (not a narrow trail), he can turn into the hill. Thus he will change direction, from going downhill to skiing horizontally or even uphill a ways, and naturally will slow down.

(3) If he is young and supple he can crouch lower and lower until his hands touch the snow, and thus stop himself. This is easy for very young people, but it is not recommended for older skiers or for those not in good training.

(4) One can slow himself by grasping both poles as one and "riding" them. This means putting the two poles (now held together as one) between the legs and bearing down on them so that the tips of the poles press into the snow and, by offering resistance, slow the skier. In using the poles as a stopping agent, there are two points which should be remembered: (a) the poles should be held against the side of the crotch, so that they are pressing against the side of the thigh and not the middle of the crotch; (b) the poles should be held at about a 60° angle to the ground—that is, so that they are more vertical than horizontal.

(5) For older skiers, a good method in soft snow is to simply collapse sideways into the snow. This is what Bill does—and, gracious knows, has done often—and he has never been hurt. Being a conservative skier, he learned this method of stopping

himself long before he went on steep hills. He practiced falling to the side fifteen or twenty times on gentle slopes in soft snow. The advantage of falling to the side is that it is easy to choose the spot to fall in more accurately. Also the skis end up in a parallel position, not all askew.

The best method of slowing, of course, is by turning with a half-plow, as described on page 56—if there is room. However, it is often necessary to resort to the other techniques.

The one important thing to remember is *never fall forward!*

Another method used for slowing—*and with a great deal of caution by some experts*—involves putting both poles out simultaneously and pushing against them. A reverse double pole, in other words. When used several times in quick succession, this can be quite effective.

Uphills: Naturally, the several steps mentioned earlier in the book are useful in resting on the uphills—i.e., the side step, the herringbone, etc. There are a few other hints. The most common mistake made by skiers is to expend so much energy fighting their way up the hill that there is none left to continue after reaching the top. The attack on the hills should be planned; energy ought to be conserved by using the head (especially since it recovers much more easily than the body). The skier should use natural terrain features, such as plateaus, to his advantage. Sometimes, and for some skiers, it is easier to climb up in deep snow (not too deep—just enough to be anti-back-slip).

There should be a minimum of *three* people even on short tours. In case of an accident, one could stay with the victim, and the other could go for help. Also, it would do well to remember that weather conditions can change *rapidly* and *radically.* Joe Pete has been in temperature changes of 20° in less than one hour.

On long tours we recommend that the skier take along ski-goggles, waterproof matches, a flashlight, and a whistle. A map and a compass are always helpful in strange territory.

The skier should never go to sleep if he is extremely cold.

If he does he probably will never wake up.

Skis or other protection should be placed under injured persons.

It is easy to be fooled when estimating the length of time required for a tour. The depth of the snow, weather, and ability account for most errors in judgment. Someone (such as the ski patrol or park ranger) should always be notified of the time an anticipated trip is to be taken as well as the *expected time of return*. The spot chosen as the departure point should be one which is used as some activity—i.e., a warming hut or a base lodge, a parking lot or someone's home, etc.

22

Odds and Ends

(1) It is always more important to force the breath out than to breathe in. The skier should concentrate on exhaling forcibly. It is probably the most effective single thing one can do to reduce the tiring effect of strenuous exercise. Racers sound like a steam engine going along. If carbon dioxide is forced out vigorously, the proper in-breathing will take care of itself, and stamina will be measurably *increased*.

(2) One must be extremely careful not to overexercise when trying out a new sport or when getting into shape after long periods of inactivity. Overtired muscles are easily injured, and the recovery period for them can be long and damaging to the health.

(3) When skiing along in a diagonal, the skier should remember to keep his hands and fingers relaxed. Just as a diver poised on the end of the diving board shakes his fingers out thus relaxing his entire body, so should the skier stay relaxed. The forward arm swing should be low and relaxed, and the back should be continually rolling from side to side with rhythm.

(4) Particular attention should be paid to the skis; the work they perform is profound and fascinating. They should be wiped off before being brought inside. The tails should not be allowed to sit in a puddle of water for they will soon warp and the laminations will separate. If storing them on the tips is the only solution, the skier should be careful to put them where they will not be stepped on or hit by a swinging door. Waxing wet skis is frustrating and usually unsuccessful.

The binding screws should be kept tight at all times. If these work loose and the binding pulls out, a skier may very well come home some day extremely fatigued and with one wet leg.

A screw driver and an extra tip (in case of a broken ski) are imperative items to take along on any tour.

If no aluminum tip is taken along, and someone on the tour can spare an extra glove or mitten, this should be slid over the tip of the broken ski. No races will be won, but it takes a lot of embarrassment out of the whole mess.

For summer storage the coolest place is best. Dampness is seldom a problem, since skis tend to become too dry during the summer. If the last application of klister is not removed, there is no need to worry about it. Since wood will assume its own natural position, we don't find any sort of blocking particularly effective. If in the fall an inexpensive ski has become badly warped, it should be thrown into the snow near the house where no one will disturb it and allowed to soak up moisture for five to ten days. Then an attempt should be made to spring it back with either weights or pressure. In time, the ski will warp again, but hopefully some use will have been gotten out of it. Often, a ski shop can help. In fall, with any cross-country skis, always bury them in the snow and allow them to soak before using them. More skis are broken the first few times out in the early season than at any other time because the skier has not moisturized the skis after the summer drying-out period.

(5) One must be extremely careful not to fall forward while skiing. It is not only dangerous, but some of the most difficult positions are attained when this happens which can make getting up practically an impossibility.

(6) Most beginners and intermediates should at least shower but preferably bathe within ten to fifteen minutes after returning from a hard tour. The point here is not to get clean but rather to relax and avoid getting chilled. Extremely sore and stiff muscles may result from catching even a slight chill while still hot and sweaty.

(7) The skier must be extremely careful when skiing with cameras or other equipment slung around the shoulders. Often, in a fall, the skier will land on such items. We recommend either a back pack or waist pack, which would provide some cushioning effect.

(8) Many times during the season, we have found that yesterday's wax works best. Each time a skier goes out, it is not necessary to clean the skis of the last application of hard wax (provided it is another hard-wax day). Once outside, if the desired effect has not been obtained, it is easy to rub something else over the existing wax. The skier should not worry about corking it in, but should rub it vigorously a few times with his glove. A couple of hundred yards on the snow will do the rest. Sometimes the tar base alone is as good as any wax that can be put on. Occasionally, klisters work this way; however, it must be remembered that they are more temperamental. When applying base wax (the skier should touch up bare spots frequently, otherwise the ski just wears out faster), the klister only has to bubble a few seconds and only in that spot immediately surrounding the area that the torch is heating. Extreme heat-

ing only serves to weaken the laminations of the ski. (For a complete run-down of this procedure, see Part IV, Chapters 24–27.)

(9) An individual should check his projected skiing area thoroughly. It is amazing where skiers and skiing can be found in the United States. Often, people feel that it is necessary to have rugged mountains and modern ski resorts, so that many exciting places are overlooked.

(10) Good care should be taken of the boots. They deserve regular applications of water-repellent preservatives and polish.

(11) The skis should always be placed outside to cool before going skiing. Many waxing and icing problems can be avoided if the skier learns to do this.

(12) It is better to go out overdressed than underdressed. The farther a person goes from his starting point, the more he is at the mercy of the elements. If an accident occurs or if weather conditions change rapidly, the skier must be prepared. Also, if the skier is wearing an overabundance of clothing, he must be intelligent about removing the proper garments at the proper time (it is often better to take off an undergarment when the wind is blowing and leave a parka on). If excess clothing is not removed soon enough, it becomes damp and unfit to put back on when conditions change again.

(13) If a skier becomes extremely tired or exhausted on the trail, he should find a comfortable spot to rest for several minutes. *After putting on an extra jacket,* he should eat some candy or take a few small drinks and should avoid getting very cold. When he starts moving again, he should concentrate on using different muscles.

(14) If a skier should get lost, it is generally best to simply go back on the track he has just made. If there are several tracks, it is easy to tell direction by checking where the pole was pulled out of the snow as the skier moved forward (it will leave a drag mark in the direction of travel; *Fig. 1*), and by

Fig. 1 checking the little ridge of snow left by each ski as it was planted and moved forward. (An experienced woodsman will tell you to go downstream if you chance on one.) It is always best to study maps when going to an unfamiliar area. The skier should be conscious of directions, should locate where the sun normally sets, and should distinguish among various prominent landmarks before starting. One must keep an eye on them—they change profoundly.

(15) Cross-country poles are longer for a reason. A skier can get away with using shorter poles such as alpine poles; this, however, is a great way to strain one's back and to never fully enjoy cross-country skiing. There is a strain on the back even with poles of the proper length.

(16) All sorts of experiments are being done with various types and lengths of skis. There has been some success with both metal and fiberglass skis, but the beginner should use a type of proven ski.

(17) A very subtle yet very important point is the flexibility of a pair of skis (*Fig.* 2). If the skis are too stiff, they will not glide well since the tip and tail are constantly acting as a brake, and this constant resistance may cause the lower leg muscles to cramp. If the ski is too limber, again the braking process comes into effect and there is no life in the ski to aid in the gliding process. This is not to say that a great deal of casual touring cannot be done without undue difficulty. The effects described become important on repeated long tours or on a hard track.

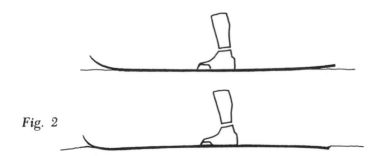

Fig. 2

(18) We strongly recommend the heel plates we described earlier (p. 21). If these are unavailable, the skier should get something—even a piece of old rubber stair-tread.

(19) If it's possible to obtain knickers we recommend they be purchased. They allow for tremendous freedom of movement and are completely satisfactory in every way.

(20) The skier should not fret about gouges or splinters. Plastic wood will fill the deep gouges satisfactorily; or, if they are not too deep simple sanding will do the job. Splinters should be glued back on or, if possible, just trimmed with a jackknife.

(21) If the poles crack, they should be taped. Occasionally, drilling a hole at the end of a crack may stop the crack from traveling; however, it is no guarantee. But taping between the joints of a bamboo pole (the type we prefer to use) with electrician's tape definitely does help. If the leather baskets are put on with wire, the wire should not be tightened excessively. The wire will wear right through the leather. These should be checked periodically so that a basket is not lost out in the woods. It is always good to take along extra leathers, baskets, and wire. We have a friend who does this and he has *never* lost a basket.

(22) When storing wax, the coolest place possible should be used; the skier should keep it out of the sun and should make sure that all containers are tightly closed. Metal boxes or plastic bags work well. The waxes should not be placed with anything one might wish to save.

(23) We have said very little about mounting bindings. There are as many theories about the mounting process as there are skiers. We mount our bindings so that the ball of the foot is just behind the balancing point of the ski, or so that approximately the middle or front of the toe piece is over the balancing point. (A rule of thumb is that the ball of the foot should be from 1½ to 2½ inches behind the balancing point. This measurement, unlike those in downhill skiing, is not critical.) The ski, when held with the fingers in the middle of the

toe plate (*Fig. 3*), will slant with the tip down. A ski shop is usually a good source of help and information as far as mounting is concerned.

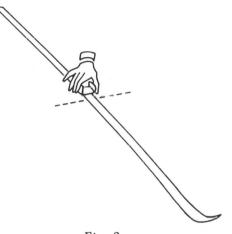

Fig. 3

(24) When confronted with obstacles, the skier should size up the situation to decide whether or not it is necessary to remove the skis. In the case of barbed-wire fences, usually the best solution is to take them off.

(25) One should be careful when skiing alone.

(26) One should not get overheated, especially on long uphills.

(27) There is one important difference between touring and racing. In racing one must maintain as rapid a tempo as possible for a long period of time. Do not attempt to keep up a fast tempo unless in good physical condition. Cross-country racing is one of the most physically exhausting of sports. Cross-country racers train by running or skiing twenty to thirty miles every day for months before the season starts. *The once-a-month racer may damage himself physically.* However, the once-a-month tourer, the one who takes his time, will derive only good health and pleasure from his tour.

This is not to say that occasional bursts of speed are wrong. Many people find great joy in combining a burst of speed with slow-or medium-speed touring. The Scandinavians will often put on a burst of speed for several hundred yards while ski touring, and this is done by older as well as younger skiers. They call it "fartlekking," which means simply varying speed and exertion along with changes in terrain, snow conditions, track conditions, and one's own personal mood. It is one of the best methods of getting into good condition. If one is already in good condition, it is best to go hard-out most of the time. This greatly increases speed and conditioning.

23

Hints for Competitive Skiing

Racing Skis and Racing Bindings

Racing skis are generally narrow, some being as narrow as 2 inches measured at the tip and tail. They have numerous laminations, are light, and are exceptionally flexible. They can be broken easily, even while being waxed.

Although racing skis provide all the support necessary in any snow conditions (even the deepest and loosest of powder snows), we do not recommend these for general touring. Even a racer should have an extra pair of training skis—generally the racing type, but they may be slightly heavier and still do no harm. After awhile a pair of skis will naturally lose some of its life and flexibility. Also, there is always the probability of breaking them, particularly when exploring in deep woods, and this expense should be avoided; therefore, the racer should have an extra pair of skis, heavier ones, for practice and for touring.

Almost all of the higher-priced racing skis are acceptable. Coaches should remember to standardize the boots and bindings purchased for their teams. It is much easier to replace a broken ski during a race when everybody has boots and bindings which are interchangeable. Some racers prefer rubber-soled boots since these can slip into many different types of bindings.

Bindings

There are many bindings on the market besides the ones that we described earlier. Most of them have some good qualities. Both Silvretta and Jofa are versatile bindings. It is a combination of touring binding and downhill binding. With the use of "downpulls" (small metal hooks on the sides of the ski under the point where the heel of the boot touches the ski) and an adjustable cable, this ski with this type of binding can be used for casual downhill skiing as well as for touring (by not using "downpulls" and by tightening the cable slightly, thereby freeing the heel).

It is an excellent binding, but designed more specifically for mountaineering rather than for cross-country. For long tours, it is slightly awkward and fatiguing to use.

Breathing

When the skier is running, he should do all of his breathing through his mouth.

This most effective method of breathing while skiing may seem to be backward to the one who is just learning it—and it is; but this is the best method. The skier should not concentrate on breathing in. We repeat—the concentration is not on the breathing in but on the breathing out (*Fig. 1*).

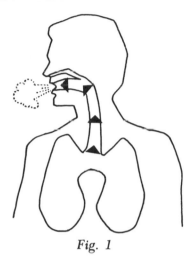

Fig. 1

The air should be emptied from the lungs with a great, big, powerful whooooossshh, thus emptying the lungs of the carbon dioxide which has accumulated from the strenuous physical exercise. *The skier should not even be thinking about breathing in.* If the air is forced out of the lungs, the lungs will draw the breath in quite naturally on their own and in a very comfortable and invigorating manner.

If the skier can acquire the habit of emptying his lungs in this manner thus getting rid of the excess carbon dioxide, the way his stamina in skiing will increase will be almost miraculous.

Advanced Uphill

The single, most important aspect of climbing a hill for a racer—providing that reasonable technique has been learned —is developing a pace at the bottom of a hill and carrying it all the way through to the top regardless of circumstance. This takes guts and determination! A good racer skis away from the top of a hill as if he were starting off on a vigorous Sunday walk.

How is a good pace developed? It is developed in part by experience and in part by a healthy attitude. The racer has to develop the idea that he is going to maintain a *constant speed* up the hill—that he is going to ski right up it no matter what. *And,* most important, that he is going to ski right away once he gets to the top.

Tempo

Pace is a very subtle thing—and every winning racer must have it. It is the sense by which the racer arrives at the finish line the moment his resources have been fully used up—not before and not after. He finishes after having used up his strength completely—and this involves his emotional and mental storehouses as well as his physical ones. But his total resources must not be used up until after he crosses the finish line. Pacing is more than tempo in that it involves both mental and physical reactions; in tempo, the reactions are purely physical ones.

No one can teach pacing to a racer. It can only be acquired through practice, practice, practice—by imagining that every practice session is the real thing.

The essence of pacing for the racer is contained in the maxim "know thyself."

Note: Tempo and pace are frequently confused terms. Tempo is the speed with which the skier moves his legs and arms at any particular moment. The tempo—which may vary—is based on the pace which the skier, consciously or unconsciously, has determined for that specific race.

Training for Racing

Cross-country racing is probably the most strenuous of sports. It involves the entire spectrum of excellent health, eating habits, muscle tone, and psychic looseness. Training for racing, therefore, is a complex, specialized subject. Because of the tremendous difference in individual racers and in coaching methods, the details of training are beyond the scope of this book. Although the only first-class instruction on this subject is still in the heads of coaches and racers, a general principle is that any program which builds muscle strength, stamina, and flexibility, combined with a regimen designed to improve breathing is good conditioning for cross-country.

PART **IV**

WAXING AND THE WIND-CHILL FACTOR

24

The Theory of Waxing

When the theory of waxing is understood, the entire "mysterious" waxing of skis becomes clear and simple.

The first thing to realize is that the ski does not slide on the snow. It slides on a thin layer of moisture which is between the snow and the ski surface. The thin layer of moisture is created by the pressure of the ski upon the snow and by the friction caused by motion across the snow. (Pressure and friction both cause heat, which melts some of the snow.)

But, it is not only necessary for the ski to slide. There must be brief moments going uphill or on the flats when the ski "locks" into the snow so that it holds still while the skier pushes the other ski forward.

This "locking in" occurs whenever the ski has weight on it and is standing still. The fact that a ski will slide easily over the snow and also provide a base from which the skier can push himself forward is a marvel largely made possible by wax.

How is it possible for the ski to lock into the snow temporarily and then resume sliding again?

It is made possible by the composition and shape of the individual snow crystals. New snowflakes have points or "arms" on them (*Fig. 1*).

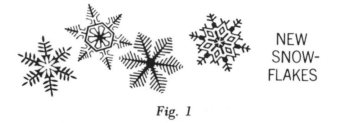

NEW SNOW-FLAKES

Fig. 1

When the ski is standing still and has weight on it, the arms of the snow crystals are pushed into the uneven surface (as it appears under the microscope) of the wax on the ski's surface. Figure 2 indicates the principle involved.

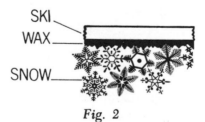

SKI
WAX
SNOW

Fig. 2

When the arms of the snowflakes take hold of the rough surface of the wax, a static friction is made. This friction keeps the ski in place as long as there is weight on the ski—the weight that is pressing the arms of the snow crystals into the crevices of the wax.

The ski is held in place to the degree that it is possible for the skier to use it as a base from which to push forward.

Naturally, the degree with which the arms of the snow crystals hold onto the wax is dependent upon three things: 1) the shape of the snow crystals; 2) the type of wax; and 3) the amount of moisture in the snow. Moisture acts as a lubricant. The layer of moisture comes between the snow and the wax on the ski. Therefore, the thickness or thinness of the layer of moisture can determine if the snow crystals and wax are close together or widely separated.

The thicker the layer of moisture, the more difficult it is for the arms of the snowflakes to reach up and grab the wax. It is more difficult because, if the layer of moisture is thick, the arms have a further distance to reach. If the layer is too thick, the arms of the snowflakes might be too short to reach out over such a distance.

Therefore, the greater the moisture content of the snow, the greater the "reaching down" quality of the wax must be. Hence, usually, the more moisture present, the rougher and stickier the wax surface must be.

Obviously, then, the moisture content of the snow is *one* of the factors influencing the kind of wax used.

And, equally obviously, the temperature of the air is *another* influencing factor. The warmer the air, the more moisture there will be—because heat releases moisture content from the crystals.

The shape of the snow crystals is *still another* factor to be considered. When the snowflakes are new, they are in their original crystalline form; and it is at this time that their arms are at their longest. The longer the snowflake points (arms) are, the more easily they can reach upward and grab onto the wax's irregular surface.

When the snowflakes are newly fallen and the weather is cold (low moisture content), the locking-in process between the snow crystals and wax is most efficient. Therefore, a hard, smooth, thin layer of wax can supply the desired locking-in friction.

If too soft a wax is used, the arms of the snowflakes will get too firm a hold on the wax—they will get "tangled up" in the wax, and the snowflakes will not be able to let go as the weight is removed from the ski and the ski is moved ahead.

Now the snow sticks to the ski, "balls up" on the ski bottom, and prevents the ski from moving forward. When this happens, the skier has to remove his skis and scrape off the snow and the wax before he can continue.

This is why, if a cross-country skier is in doubt, he will tend to wax "too hard." It is easy to put soft wax over hard wax; but the opposite is impossible in most snow conditions, and difficult under any.

Up until now, we have been speaking only of the newly fallen snow—where the snow crystals still maintain their original form.

But, shortly after the snow has fallen (between twenty-four and thirty-six hours), especially if there are temperature variations, the points (long arms) of the snow crystals begin to wear off and become shorter.

As days go by, the snow crystals become smoother and smoother. For this reason, "old snow" is more slippery than "new snow," and, therefore, a softer, thicker wax must be used to make it easier for the now smoother crystals to grab onto the wax (*Fig. 3*).

OLD
SNOW-
FLAKES

Fig. 3

With time and sun, further changes take place to the snow crystals. The crystals melt into each other and become tiny pellets of ice which do not have the long points or arms with which to hold onto the wax surface.

This is corn snow or other variations of snowflakes turned into ice.

Corn snow requires a still softer, stickier wax; and the warmer the weather, the greater the moisture content, which requires an even stickier, softer, thicker form of wax.

Generally, the snow which has changed to some form of ice —slush, heavy ice crystals, corn snow, crust, or packed ice— requires the stickiest of all waxes—the liquid waxes which are called klister waxes. But more about them later.

A *résumé of the waxing theory:* A ski which is properly waxed will slide easily along the snow as long as the ski is moving or has no weight on it. Under these conditions, the arms or points of the snow crystals cannot lock into the wax on the ski's surface.

Once the ski stops moving and has weight upon it, it becomes temporarily locked into the snow. It is this locking in which permits the skier to push himself ahead of the other ski.

When the temporarily locked-in ski is unweighted, it then becomes unlocked and can slide easily.

When the ski is moving or is unweighted, the arms of the snow crystals cannot fasten themselves into the wax, and the ski—on a thin layer of moisture—slides easily ahead.

25

Preparing the Ski Bottom

It was mentioned earlier in Chapter 2 ("Beginner's Check-Off Equipment List") that the bottom surface of the ski must be treated, and it was suggested that this first be done at the shop where the skis were bought.

Here is the procedure in detail, should the skier wish to do the job himself.

The bottom surface of the ski requires a base preparation. The base preparation has three functions: 1) to waterproof the bottom ski surface; 2) to protect the bottom of the ski against abrasion; and 3) to provide a surface to which the waxes can adhere.

There are three types of base preparations: 1) the impregnation type; 2) the base-wax type; and 3) the tar treatment.

Impregnation type (not recommended for serious skiers—unless they are in a hurry): This includes Swix Aerosol and Østbye Mixol. These are easy to apply, either by spraying or by putting them on with a paint brush. The impregnation material will waterproof the ski bottom excellently, but wax does not adhere to it as well as to the other substances which follow below.

Base wax (recommended only for special racing conditions): These include Swix Orange, Rex Orange, Rode Nera, Toko, and Rode Chola. Base waxes are not recommended for the average cross-country skier and ski tourer. True, other waxes adhere well to the base wax, but the application of base waxes must be done frequently and adds one more complication which is not necessary except occasionally for cross-country racing. We have learned, for example, that on new Arctic snow (extremely dry snow) when the temperature is −10° F. or below, Rex Light Green applied over a *very* thin layer of base wax seemed to increase our speed slightly. Such preparation is not needed except for competitive racing under special conditions, or for the cross-country skier who just wants to experiment. We tried this out and found that although speed on the flats and downhill was increased slightly, it increased fatigue in the long uphill pulls (for some reason this wax combination had a reduced holding effect thus requiring a slightly deeper crouch and a slightly harder slap-down of the skis to keep a constant speed going uphill).

Tar preparations (recommended): Tar preparations protect the ski excellently and also form an effective adhesive for the wax. We recommend that tar-base preparations be used by all cross-country skiers for all general conditions. We recommend that the tar preparation which requires burning in be used. Almost all professional and expert cross-country skiers prefer the burned-in tar treatment. It is more trouble than other methods and is a dirtier job, but it functions better and lasts longer than other base preparations.

There are also some tar preparations which do not have to

be burned in. These are either sprayed on or painted on. They are Swix Special, Rex Rapid Tar, Haka Rapid Tar, Toko Grundvalla, and Østbye Aerosol. These are satisfactory for the skier who does not ski very much, but we recommend the burned-in tars for the serious skier.

How to apply "burn in" tar-base preparations: There are three burn-in tars easily available in the United States: 1) Rode Grundvalla; 2) Swix Wallco; and 3) Holmenkol.

The equipment required includes the tar preparation, a blowtorch or a gas torch, some rags (plenty of them), as well as lots of newspapers on the floor. We prefer the gas torch. It is lighter and easier to handle.

The skis are placed in a steady position, bottom sides up

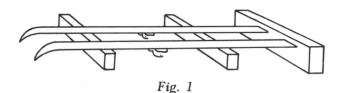

Fig. 1

(*Fig. 1*). Some people place the skis across two sawhorses with the tails against the wall so that the skis will not slip. A professional we know puts the skis against a workbench at a 45° angle, and then holds them steady by means of a vise.

The bottoms of the skis must be clean and sanded down to the bare wood.

Important: Almost all new skis coming from the factory have a protective coating on the bottoms. This protective coating must be removed before putting on any base preparation. It is easy to sandpaper off. *A light sandpapering is all that is required.*

The tar preparation is spread over the ski bottoms with either a stick, rag, or preferably a paintbrush as the spreader.

The individual should take the blowtorch or the gas torch and, starting at one end of the skis, should heat the tar until it

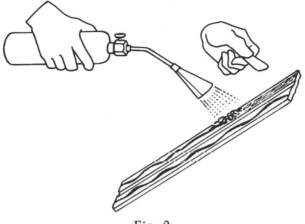

Fig. 2

bubbles, gradually going down the length of the skis until the entire tarred surface has been "boiled" (*Fig. 2*). He should not get excited if the tar begins to burn a little; it will go out on its own quickly.

The only hazard is burning the wooden base of the skis. There is little danger of this, however, as long as the flame is kept moving back and forth.

After the tar on both skis has been burned in, the process is then repeated, only this time, the tar is wiped off just after it has been "boiled" for the second time.

The skier should "boil" a few inches of it, holding the torch in the right hand; then, taking the torch away, he should wipe it with the rags.

This should be kept up until the entire ski surface has been treated.

The skis should be allowed to stand for several hours at room temperature, and they will then be ready for the other waxes. To know if a sufficient amount of tar base has been applied, one's finger, if gently pressed on the surface, should just barely stick to the bottom.

Caution: This process should not be done to skis with plastic bottoms.

Today, in 1972, there are newly developed skis with plastic bottoms. Others have synthetic wooden bases. Each manufacturer gives specific, and often unique instructions for preparing (and later waxing) the ski bottoms. *These special instructions must be read,* particularly regarding the application of heat. Excessive heat can ruin a plastic or synthetic ski.

Note: We recommend that all new cross-country skiers start out with ordinary wooden cross-country skis which have birch or hickory bottoms. Birch holds wax better, but the harder hickory will last longer.

Experiments on skis with plastic bottoms should be avoided until the advanced-intermediate or expert level has been reached.

26

Knowing Which Wax to Use

For waxing, we will take into consideration the three general conditions of snow timewise (by timewise, we mean the length of time the snow has been on the earth): 1) falling snow and new snow; 2) settled snow; and 3) snow which has turned into some form of ice.

Pages 177–179 have separate scales for each of the above three kinds of snow. This has been done in detail so that the skier can see that there is no mystery at all about selecting the right wax. It *mostly* concerns accurate identification of snow conditions. In these three tables which follow, Table I is for falling snow; Table II is for settled snow; and Table III is for snow which has turned into ice.

There are six types of snow to be considered: 1) extremely dry snow (Arctic snow); 2) very dry snow (mountain snow); 3) dry snow; 4) transition snow (that which is in the process of turning from snow crystals into ice crystals); 5) mushy snow; and 6) wet snow.

The various types of snow usually occur within certain temperature ranges. The temperature range (see the tables) will give a pretty good idea as to snow type. But this is not always entirely accurate because, often, the wind influences snow structure; and, also, if the temperature is changing, the change in snow temperature may lag behind that in air temperature.

Therefore, the air temperature should be measured to see in which category the snow probably lies. Then, a handful of snow should be picked up and given the test indicated in the tables. Having thus identified the snow type, one should then see which kind of wax is required for that particular type of snow.

The waxes are usually identified by color.

In the tables, the color (type) wax applicable is shown beneath the name of the company which manufactures it—Rex, Swix, etc.

There are solid waxes and liquid waxes.

Most of the time (*but not always*), if the temperature is below 32° F. or 0° C., solid waxes are used exclusively. The solid waxes come in round containers, about 2 inches long and about 1¼ inches in diameter. The color of the solid wax is the same as the color of the container.

The container is made of a lead substance which is easily peeled off as more and more wax is used from the top (*Fig. 1*).

Fig. 1

After the container has been opened, one should always save the top, and put it back on after using some of the wax. This prevents dirt from getting into the wax and also stops the wax from smudging clothing, wax kits, etc. Printed on the outside of the container are the temperature ranges and snow conditions for which the wax should be used. These are good, adequate instructions. We have made the tables mostly to help the skier learn how to identify the snow conditions.

The colder the conditions are, the harder the wax to be used. After having read the theory of waxing, the skier should know the reason for this, including the exception of using the oozy blue klister on ice.

When the temperature for new or falling snow is above 32° F. or 0° C. (*note:* the temperature now is *above* the freezing point), the snow surface usually becomes more slippery than when it is below the freezing point. Under these conditions, a sticky, liquid wax is used.

This extremely sticky, liquid wax is called *klister*. Klister is identified by color in the same way as solid waxes. Thus, we have red klister, yellow klister, blue klister, and so forth.

The klister (liquid) wax usually comes in a tube. It looks like a toothpaste tube. It is about 5 inches long and about 1¼ inches in diameter. The tube has a screw-on top. One must be certain to always put the top back on immediately after use (*Fig. 2*).

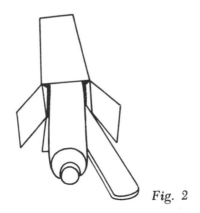

Fig. 2

Klister is oozy stuff and, if it is left in a warm place, can ooze out and make an awful mess.

(*Note:* At the end of the season, if there is any klister left in the tubes, one should make certain that the tops are on tight. Also, he should make certain that the tubes are put in several paper bags or a tight tin box. In very hot weather, the klister is apt to ooze from the opened container whether the top is well screwed on or not. Sometimes it leaks from the bottom if the tube has been partially used.)

The first step is to identify the snow conditions and choose the right wax from one of the three tables. (*Note:* There is on the market an "all purpose" wax. It is a rather sticky wax which comes in a roll (not a tube, like klister). Its effectiveness comes from knowing precisely what thickness of all-purpose wax to apply to the ski. We know some experienced ski-tourers who go out with nothing but a tube of all-purpose wax and a square of paraffin. But these skiers are experts and have had a lot of experience with the all-purpose wax. We do *not* recommend this for beginners. One might experiment with it for fun if desired, but should first become familiar with the regular waxes and klisters. Paraffin is a good thing to take on a tour. If under certain conditions [usually old snow about 32° F.] the snow ices and balls up on the ski, an emergency measure is to take off old wax and put on the paraffin.

Toko is attempting to simplify waxing by offering two all-purpose waxes. At this writing, they have not been tested for American snow conditions.

TABLE I

FALLING (OR NEW) SNOW

(GENERALLY, SNOW WHICH HAS BEEN ON THE GROUND LESS THAN 24 TO 36 HOURS)

Snow Type	Temperature Range C.	Temperature Range F.	Rex Wax	Swix Wax	Helmenkol Wax	Rode Wax
Arctic Snow (extremely dry snow): When it is falling, it looks like powdered sugar. It is fine. When a handful of it is picked up and blown, it blows out of the hand like smoke.	−10° and below	14° and below	Light Green	Green	Green	Light Green
Mountain Snow (very dry snow): When blown, the slightest puff will send the snow swirling from the hand, but not as easily as Arctic snow.	−7° and below	20° and below	Green	Green	Green	Green
Normal Dry Snow: One has to puff hard to move it by blowing.	−7°–1°	20°–30°	Blue	Blue	Blue	Blue
Transition Snow: When picked up, it will tend to form loose lumps in the hand. It will not blow away no matter how hard one puffs.	−1°–2°	30°–35°	Purple	Purple	Purple	Purple
Mushy Snow: Not only will this snow lump in the hand, but if lumps are pushed over a snow surface, they will easily form snowballs.	0°–3°	32°–37°	Yellow	Red Klister	Violet	Yellow
Wet Snow: When picked up, the slightest pressure will cause the snow to ooze moisture.	2° and up	35° and up	Red Klister	Red Klister	Yellow Klister	Red Klister

From 35° F. (2° C.) up to 40° F. (4.4° C.): Occasionally, hard red wax will hold here; and it is worthwhile to experiment before applying the sticky klister. *Note*: This is for new snow only.

TABLE II

Settled Snow

(Snow which has been on the ground for more than 24 to 36 hours)

Snow Type	Temperature Range		Rex	Swix	Holmenkol	Rode
	C.	F.				
Mountain Snow (very dry): The snow will blow away the same as a handful of granulated sugar.	−8° and below	17° and below	Green Wax (special Green below 14° F.)	Green Wax	Green Wax	Green Wax
Dry Snow: This will form loose snowballs if packed in the hands, but will separate if dropped.	−10°−−1°	14°−30°	Blue Wax	Blue Wax	Blue Wax	Blue Wax
Transition Snow: A close look will show that this snow has begun to turn into ice crystals. When the hand is closed on the snow, the crystals will adhere in tight clumps.	−2°−1°	29°−34°	Purple (Violet) Wax	Purple Wax	Purple (Violet) Wax	Purple (Violet) Wax
Wet Snow: This is sloppy slush.	2° and up	35° and up	Red Klister	Purple Klister	Yellow Klister	Red Klister

We believe the preceding waxing tables are the best possible guides to waxing; but for those who wish the traditional graphic chart, we have researched and developed the latest one, which appears below. This is for the most easily obtainable waxes: Swix, Rex, and Rode.

TABLE III

SNOW WHICH HAS TURNED INTO ICE, CRUST, OR PACKED-ICE PELLETS
(USUALLY OLD SNOW)

Snow Type	Temperature Range C.	F.	Rex Klister	Swix Klister	Holmenkol Klister	Rode Klister
Dry, Crusty Snow (also ice)	−5° and below	23° and below	Blue	Blue	Blue	Blue
Soft-Crust Snow	−5° – −1°	23°–31°	Blue	Blue	Blue	Blue
Mushy-Crust Snow	0°–1°	32°–34°	Purple	Purple	Purple	Purple
Wet Slush	0° and up	32° and up	Silver	Purple	Silver	Silver

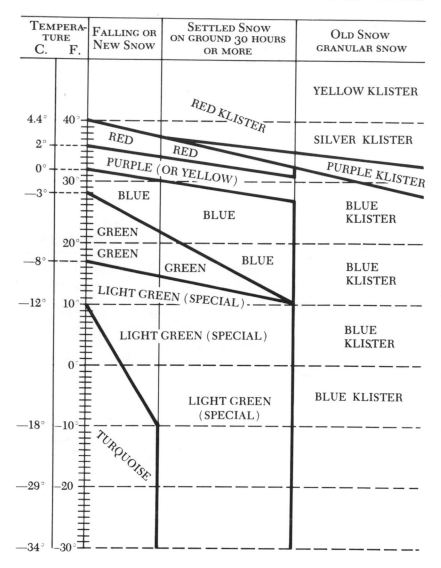

TEMPERA-TURE C. F.		FALLING OR NEW SNOW	SETTLED SNOW ON GROUND 30 HOURS OR MORE	OLD SNOW GRANULAR SNOW
				YELLOW KLISTER
4.4°	40°		RED KLISTER	
2°		RED	RED	SILVER KLISTER
0°		PURPLE (OR YELLOW)		PURPLE KLISTER
−3°	30°	BLUE	BLUE	BLUE KLISTER
	20°	GREEN		
−8°		GREEN	GREEN BLUE	BLUE KLISTER
−12°	10°	LIGHT GREEN (SPECIAL)		
			LIGHT GREEN (SPECIAL)	BLUE KLISTER
	0°			
			LIGHT GREEN (SPECIAL)	BLUE KLISTER
−18°	−10°	TURQUOISE		
−29°	−20°			
−34°	−30°			

27

Applying and Removing Wax

It is preferable to have the skis at room temperature and the waxes chilled. The roll of wax should be placed outside for a half an hour before using. (We are speaking of waxes, *not* klisters.)

The skier should decide which wax is to be used. If he is in doubt, he should put on the harder of the two waxes. If the harder of the two is too slippery on the snow, it is easy to put a layer of softer wax over it. It should be remembered, however, that hard waxes cannot be put over softer waxes effectively.

We repeat, if in doubt, the harder of the two waxes should be used.

How to Apply Wax

The waxes, in order of hardness, are as follows (the hardest wax at the top, becoming softer as they go to the end of the list): Light Green; Green; Blue; Purple (or Yellow); and Red.

The most common method of applying wax is to place the tail of the ski against a wall (where the wall and the floor meet). The individual should hold the ski in the left hand and apply the wax from the container to the ski surface with the

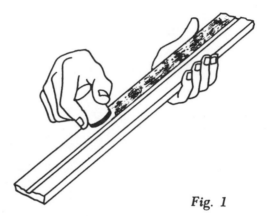

Fig. 1

right. With an up and down motion, the wax is rubbed on the ski bottom, completely covering the surface (*Fig. 1*).

Then, the individual should take a ski cork (*Fig. 2*)—this is what it is called, even though some types no longer are made of cork; it can be purchased wherever wax is sold—and using the cork as a buffer, he should smooth down the wax on the

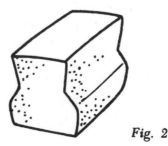

Fig. 2

ski bottom. When the corking is completed, the wax should have a thin, shiny look. This is the simplest and most common method.

Many instructors or coaches will apply the wax as described above, then run a torch over it to melt it and have it glide smoothly without corking. Some racers prefer smoothing the wax on by ironing it—using an electric traveling iron. This guarantees a very thin, even wax coat. Others will pass the flame of a torch over the wax and then spread the still-melted wax out with a paintbrush.

A new device, the "Skiwaxer," soon will be available and is excellent. Primus makes a similar product.

If there are *many* skis to be waxed, the easiest method is to melt some of the wax in a pot, and apply melted wax directly to the ski bottom with a paintbrush.

But most ski tourers smooth the wax by the simple method of rubbing it with a cork. It is easy, effective, and requires little equipment.

After the wax has been applied and smoothed, the skis should be placed out of doors to let the wax cool to outdoor temperature. Ten to fifteen minutes is sufficient.

The skis now are ready for use.

Before going on a tour, the individual should try the skis out for several hundred yards. It takes about ten minutes of use on the snow for the wax to "mature." It is only then that the skier can tell whether he has used the right wax or not. If in doubt, he should try going up a slope to see if the wax holds. If the ski slips, the wax is too hard. If the ski seems to resist the snow when moving forward, the wax is too soft.

For the beginner, it is better to have the wax a bit slow (or sticky) than too fast (or slippery).

Usually only one *thin* layer of wax is required, but when going on a long tour or if the snow is scratchy, a thicker wax coating may be desirable. In this case, several thin layers are better than one thick one. Put a thin layer on, let it cool outside, then apply another layer.

How to Apply Klister

The skier should have both the klister and the skis at room temperature if possible.

The skis are positioned against the wall in the same way as when applying wax.

The individual should now open the tube of klister but should watch out since it may start oozing as soon as the top is removed. The tube is held at right angles to the ski surface and is squeezed a little. Moving it down the length of the ski (first on one side of the groove, and then on the other), small dots of klister should be placed on the surface about an inch

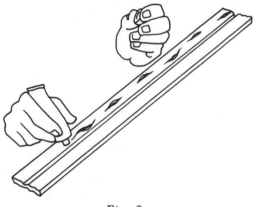

Fig. 3

apart and in a zigzag pattern (*Fig. 3*). Another method is to hold the tube at a slight angle, squeeze it, and quickly draw a thin zigzag line of klister the length of the ski (*Fig. 4*).

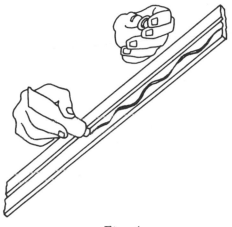

Fig. 4

The klister should be smoothed with the cork.

The method just described is used by most cross-country skiers and works well.

A quicker and more efficient method, if the equipment is available, is to apply the klister, and then heat it with a torch so that the klister melts and is smooth instead of lumpy. To get the smoothest application of klister, it should be melted with a torch and spread with a small paintbrush.

Another method is to apply the klister and then smooth it by running a hot iron up and down the bottom of the ski. A small traveling iron works well.

The klister should not be put in the groove. It should also be kept off the sides of the ski. Having it either on the sides or in the groove may result in the icing up of the snow on the ski and the inevitable slowing down of the skier.

How to Remove Wax

Many skiers scrape the hard waxes off the ski, using a simple scraper which can be purchased wherever wax is sold (*Fig. 5*).

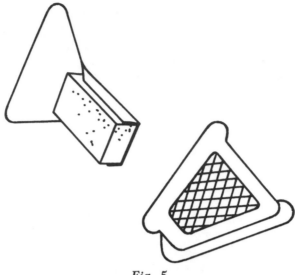

Fig. 5

Another method is to scrape off the wax, then heat what is left with a torch and wipe it off with a rag.

Rex and Toko sell ski-wax removers, wax solvents which are efficient and easy to use. A thin layer of the ski-wax remover is smoothed over the wax and allowed to stand for a few minutes. The wax can then be wiped off with a rag.

Also gasoline, paint thinner, kerosene, or a dry-cleaning fluid can be used.

When using a solvent to remove wax, the ski should be allowed to dry for fifteen or twenty minutes before putting on new wax.

How to Remove Klister

One should either use a solvent as described above, or heat the klister with a torch and then wipe it off with rags.

It is possible to scrape klister off, but it is a sticky and inefficient method.

When removing klister, one should make certain that it is also off the sides and out of the groove. Having bits of klister on the sides of ski (especially when the skier is in snow that does not require klister) attracts the snow which balls up there and, in time, can impede forward motion.

28

Wind-Chill Factor Chart

The wind-chill factor is an element with which the serious skier should become familiar (see the table on p. 188). The es-

TABLE IV.   WIND-CHILL FACTOR

	Temperature (Farenheit)												
	35	30	25	20	15	10	5	0	−5	−10	−15	−20	−25	−30
5	33	27	21	16	12	7	1	−6	−11	−15	−20	−26	−31	−35
10	21	16	9	2	−2	−9	−15	−22	−27	−31	−38	−45	−52	−58
15	16	11	1	−6	−11	−18	−25	−33	−40	−45	−51	−60	−65	−70
20	12	3	−4	−9	−17	−24	−32	−40	−46	−52	−60	−68	−76	−81
25	7	0	−7	−15	−22	−29	−37	−45	−52	−58	−67	−75	−83	−89
30	5	−2	−11	−18	−26	−33	−41	−49	−56	−63	−70	−78	−87	−94
35	3	−4	−13	−20	−27	−35	−43	−52	−60	−67	−72	−83	−90	−98
40	1	−5	−15	−22	−29	−36	−45	−54	−62	−69	−76	−87	−94	−101

Wind Velocity (miles per hour)

sence of the wind-chill factor is that when the wind is blowing, the temperature which affects the skier is actually lower than is indicated on the thermometer.

This table indicates the "effective temperature" on the human body for the various combinations of temperature and wind. For example, at 0° F. with a 15 mph. wind, the body will suffer the same heat loss as it would if the wind were −35° F. and the wind velocity were zero. Therefore, the skier should dress accordingly.